Kids Knitting

melanie falick

Photographs by
Chris Hartlove

Illustrations by
Kristin Nicholas

artisan *new york*

**For Mom, Auntie Lee, and Nanny Sophie,
my first knitting teachers**

Published by Artisan
A Division of Workman Publishing Company, Inc.
225 Varick Street, New York, NY 10014-4381
www.artisanbooks.com

Published simultaneously in Canada by Thomas Allen & Son, Limited

LIBRARY OF CONGRESS CATALOGING-IN-PUBLICATION DATA
Falick, Melanie.
    Kids Knitting : projects for kids of all ages / Melanie Falick ; photographs by Chris Hartlove ; illustrations by Kristen Nicholas.
      p. cm.
    Includes index.
    Summary: Provides step-by-step instructions covering the basic stitches, knitting tools, and finger-knitting, with directions for twelve easy projects.
    ISBN 1-885183-76-3 (hc)
    ISBN 978-1-57965-241-8 (pb)
    1. Knitting–Juvenile Literature. [1.Knitting.] I. Hartlove, Chris, ill. II. Nicholas, Kristin, ill. III. Title
TT820.F15 1998
746.43'2-dc21

                                                   97-44817
                                                       CIP
                                                       AC

Printed in Malaysia

20 19 18 17 16 15 14 13 12

First paperback edition, 2003

Book design by Susi Oberhelman

contents

Have you ever looked closely at your mittens, hats, and sweaters and wondered how they were made? There is a good chance they were knit. Knitting is a way of connecting small loops of yarn to create a fabric. The fabric can be flat, like a scarf, or it can be tubular like a hat.

No one knows exactly how long knitting has been practiced. Pieces of knit socks from between 1200 and 1400 AD have been found in Egypt—so knitting may be nearly a thousand years old, maybe even older. Until the late 1500s all knitting was done by hand. Then a knitting machine was invented, and people started to use it to make clothing more quickly. But people have never stopped knitting by hand

because it's lots of fun, useful, and easy.

In this book you will learn all you need to know to make your own hats, scarves, and sweaters, plus other fun stuff like dolls, bean bags, a bookmark, socks, a purse, even a backpack. Knitting for yourself is exciting, and so is knitting for others. Imagine the look on your mom's or sister's face when you hand her a homemade purse. What will your dad or brother say when you give him a hat created especially for him in his favorite color? Would your friends like to play with handknit bean bags?

When you learn how to knit you begin a journey that can continue all your life. Knitting is a hobby that you can do alone or with others, indoors or outdoors—at home, on the bus to school, or while listening to music or watching TV. And you can make just about anything you want once you learn the skills presented in this book. Right- and left-handed knitters can follow the same instructions because the knitting style presented here uses both hands equally. Knitting is not hard, but it does take practice, especially in the begin- ning, so be patient. If you know more experienced knitters, you can always ask them for help (if you don't know any, see page 13). If they tell you to do something differently than the instruc- tions presented here, either ask them to read these instructions or try their way. There are a few different knitting styles. It's good to be open to all of them.

Kids Knitting includes 12 knitting projects plus related activities like making your own knitting needles, dye- ing yarn with Kool-Aid, and making felt balls. There are also special features about the animals and plants whose fiber is used to make yarn, how that fiber is turned into yarn, and knitting in different parts of the world.

All of the photographs in this book were taken at Morehouse Farm in New York State. The models' names are Sasha, Emily, Manon, Nick, Stanley, Molly, and Abigail, plus Boris the llama and Sage the dog. We had a great time putting *Kids Knitting* together. Now we hope you have a great time knitting!

getting started

Yarn—in the beginning, that's all you need to learn how to knit. Before you ever pick up a pair of needles, you can start knitting on your fingers or on a spool. Both techniques can be mastered in about a minute. What's important to remember is that whether you are knitting with your fingers, with a spool, or with needles, you are always doing the same thing: connecting a series of loops. But just as a painter works with paints and brushes, a knitter works with yarns and needles. In the next few pages you'll learn how to dye your own yarn, make your own needles, and identify the tools of the knitting trade.

knitting tools you will need right away

yarn

Make sure that you absolutely love the yarn you choose because you will be spending a lot of time with it—looking at it and working with it. Make sure you love the color and also the way it feels in your hands. Bulky and worsted-weight wool are 2 good choices for beginners. Wool is the name of the fiber that grows on sheep. The words "bulky" and "worsted-weight" refer in a very general way to the thickness of the yarn. Bulky (also known as chunky) and worsted-weight, which is slightly thinner than bulky, are 2 of the most popular types of yarn, so there are a lot of choices within these 2 groups. A lot of people like to learn with acrylic yarn, which is made from synthetic fiber, because it is less expensive than wool and is machine washable (most wool needs to be washed by hand). It's also easy to find in large general merchandise stores and in arts and crafts stores. For wool, you usually need to go to a store that specializes in yarn.

straight knitting needles

Knitting needles come in many different sizes—from short to long and skinny to fat. They can be straight or circular. Straight needles can have a knob on 1 end and a point at the other or they can have points on both ends. Different sizes of needles are assigned different numbers. The skinniest needles are given the lowest numbers, such as 1, 2, and 3. The fattest needles are given the highest numbers, such as 15, 16, and 17. The size of the needles plus the thickness of the yarn and the looseness or tightness with which you knit will determine the look and feel of the finished fabric. A good choice for beginners is 10-inch-long straight needles (with knobs on one end) in any size between 6 and 10. You can buy knitting needles or you can make them yourself (see page 21).

scissors

You will need scissors that are sharp enough to cut yarn easily.

knitting tools you may need later on

tape measure or ruler

Either a tape measure or ruler can be used when measuring a flat piece of knitted fabric, but only a tape measure can be used to measure around a person's body, such as when you are trying to decide on the correct size for a sweater.

yarn needle

A yarn needle, also called a tapestry or darning needle, looks like an oversized sewing needle—except the tip is not as pointy. It's used to sew pieces of knitting together and to weave loose ends of yarn into the knitted fabric.

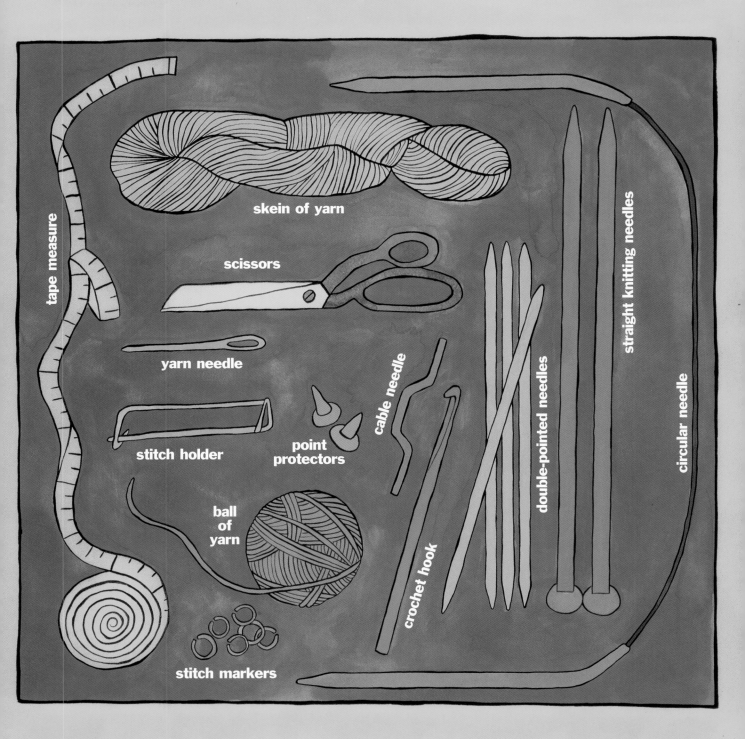

skein of yarn

scissors

yarn needle

stitch holder

point protectors

ball of yarn

stitch markers

tape measure

cable needle

crochet hook

double-pointed needles

straight knitting needles

circular needle

stitch holder

Sometimes when you're knitting you need to set a few stitches aside for a little while. To keep your knitting from unraveling, you put these stitches on a holder. Some holders look like barrettes and some look like big safety pins. If you do not have a traditional stitch holder, you can use something else in its place, such as a piece of yarn in a different color, a shoelace, or even a knitting needle with a rubber band wound around the tip so that the stitches are blocked by the band and cannot fall off.

stitch markers

Stitch markers are colored rings (usually plastic) that you place in between stitches on the knitting needle to help you keep track of what they are doing. If you do not have store-bought stitch markers, use tiny rubber bands instead (like the ones orthodontists give to patients with braces).

point protectors

Point protectors are caps that you place on the tips of knitting needles to keep stitches from falling off when they are not being knit, such as when you put a piece of knitting aside for awhile.

crochet hook

This tool looks like the average knitting needle except that it is usually shorter and it has a hook on 1 end. It is used to pick up dropped stitches. A dropped stitch is one that has fallen off the needle by accident—if you do not pick it up, you will end up with a hole in your work. Like knitting needles, crochet hooks come in many different sizes. Size G or H will work well for picking up dropped stitches for projects in this book, but other sizes can be used if you don't have a G or H on hand.

double-pointed knitting needles

These needles are straight and have points on both ends. Four or 5 of them are used at the same time to knit tubular shapes, such as socks.

circular knitting needles

Circular needles look like 2 short straight needles with a flexible plastic cord in the middle. Like double-pointed needles, they are used to knit tubular shapes. They can also be used to knit flat pieces.

cable needle

A cable needle is a short double-pointed needle that may be curved in the middle or at the end (making it look like a large hook). It is used to make cables, a group of stitches that are twisted around each other and look like rope.

Where to Go For Help if No One at Home Knits

It is often easier to learn how to knit when you have a more experienced person around to help you. If no one in your family knits, don't worry. Instead, think about other people you might ask. Knitters are usually very happy to help each other.

- Ask your parents, sisters, and brothers if they know anyone who knits, such as a neighbor or family friend.
- Ask your schoolteachers if they know how to knit.
- If you belong to a church, temple, mosque, or other community organization, ask if anyone there likes to knit.
- If you are involved in Girl Scouts or Boy Scouts, ask your troop leaders if they knit.
- Call your local 4-H club and ask if they offer any knitting classes.
- Look in the Yellow Pages for a yarn shop in your area. Yarn shops are listed under Yarn, Crafts, Craft Supplies, or Arts and Crafts. The salespeople in these shops are usually very helpful.

- Find out if there is a knitting guild in your area by contacting the Knitting Guild of America (502 Gay Street, Suite 410, Knoxville, TN 37902; (615) 524-2401). A knitting guild is a club for people who like to knit.

kool-aid yarn

This is a really fun project that does not require any special materials. All you need is 1 or more skeins of undyed wool yarn, water, white vinegar, a cooking pot or glass jar, and Kool-Aid powder. In each pot or jar, you can put 1 flavor of Kool-Aid powder or you can mix 2 or more flavors. For example, straight cherry powder will dye the yarn red, while a mixture of cherry and lemonade powder will give you more of an orange color.

Often, a skein of yarn is twisted into a figure-8. To dye the yarn, you will need to open the figure-8, which will leave you with a coil of yarn (like those shown in the photograph at left). To keep the yarn from tangling, loosely tie the coil in 4 places with a piece of undyed yarn or string (the coil may already be tied in 1 or 2 places). If you tie the coil too tightly you will end up with undyed streaks where the yarn was tied.

Undyed wool can range in color from nearly white to gray to brown. When dyeing with Kool-Aid, use white or light gray wool. That way you'll get nice bright colors.

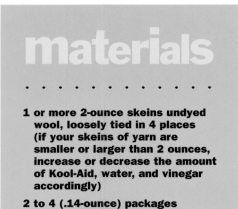

materials

. . . .

- 1 or more 2-ounce skeins undyed wool, loosely tied in 4 places (if your skeins of yarn are smaller or larger than 2 ounces, increase or decrease the amount of Kool-Aid, water, and vinegar accordingly)
- 2 to 4 (.14-ounce) packages unsweetened Kool-Aid powder for every 2 ounces of yarn (the more Kool-Aid you use the darker the final color)
- ¼ cup white vinegar for every 2 ounces of yarn

directions

stove method

1. Place the yarn in a bowl of cold water and let it sit for approximately 30 minutes.

2. Stir together the Kool-Aid, ½ gallon cold water for each 2 ounces of yarn, and the vinegar in a pot large enough to hold both the liquid and the yarn without crowding. Place the presoaked yarn in the pot.

3. Bring the mixture to a low simmer and continue to simmer for 15 to 30 minutes, until the water is clear. Clear water means all the color has been absorbed by the yarn. Let the yarn sit in the water until it cools to room temperature.

4. To rinse, fill a large bowl with room-temperature water, add the room-temperature yarn, and very gently squeeze the yarn. Repeat with fresh water until the water stays clear.

5. Hang the yarn to dry.

sun method

1. Place the yarn in a bowl of warm water and let it sit for approximately 30 minutes.

2. Stir together the Kool-Aid, ½ gallon warm water for each 2 ounces of yarn, and the vinegar in a glass jar large enough to hold the liquid and the yarn without crowding. Place the presoaked yarn in the jar. Put the cover on the jar.

3. Place the jar in a warm, sunny spot and let it sit until the water is clear. The warmer the spot, the quicker this will happen.

4. To rinse, fill a large bowl with warm water, add the yarn, and very gently squeeze the yarn. Repeat with fresh water until the water stays clear.

5. Hang the yarn to dry.

winding yarn into a ball

Some yarn is sold in a coil or figure-8 shape called a skein (rhymes with "rain"). If you try to knit from the skein, the yarn will get tangled. Before knitting, it should be rewound into a ball. Untwist the figure-8 so that it looks like a big loop. Place the loop around a friend's outstretched arms or around the back of a chair. With scissors, cut off any short pieces of yarn that are holding the separate strands together. Find the end of the yarn and begin winding it loosely around all of your fingers except for your thumb. After winding about 25 times, slip the yarn off your fingers, grab it in the center, and begin winding loosely in another direction. Wind about 25 more times, then change directions again. Continue winding and changing directions until you reach the end of the yarn.

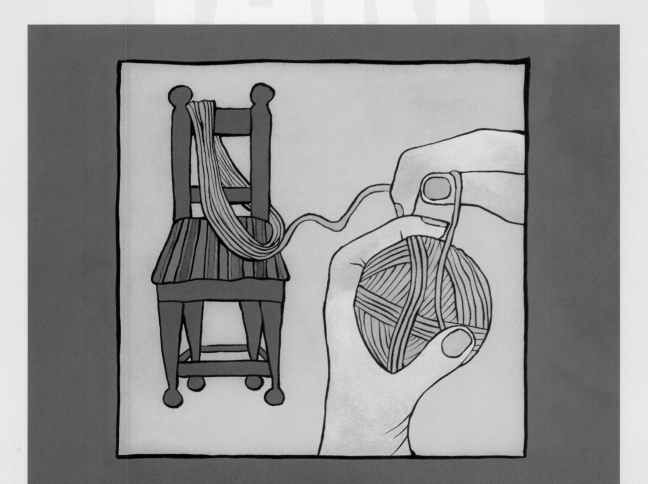

finger knitting

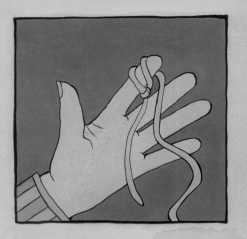

Before you start knitting with needles, spend a few minutes trying finger knitting. The springy finger-knit chains can be used as hair ribbons, bows for wrapping presents, friendship bracelets, or anklets.

1 Tie the yarn at the beginning of your ball around your index finger. Face your palm up and let the tail (the short end of the yarn) fall into your palm. Wrap the working yarn (the yarn coming from the ball) in a circle so that you have a strand of yarn wrapped above the tied yarn on your index finger. The working yarn should now be close to where it started.

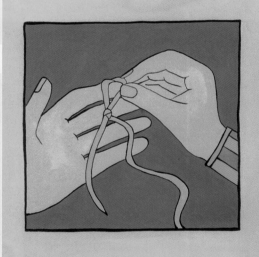

2 With the fingers of your other hand, lift the bottom loop over the top loop and drop it off the back of your finger. Repeat steps 1 and 2 several times. You will see that a knitted chain is quickly forming. Continue until the chain is as long as you want it to be.

3 To finish, cut the working yarn a few inches from the end of the chain. Push the end of the yarn through the last loop and pull tightly.

spOol knitting

Spool knitting, also known as French knitting, creates strong cords

that can be used in the same ways as finger-knit chains.

Spool-knit cord can also be used as drawstrings on bags or edgings for pillows, or can

be coiled and glued to circles of cardboard to make coasters.

1 Thread the spool by dropping the end of the yarn down the hole in the center. Hold the spool and the end of the yarn tightly with 1 hand while using the other to loop the working yarn (the yarn coming from the ball) firmly around each of the spokes 1 time. Loop all of the spokes in the same direction (either clockwise or counterclockwise), one after another.

2 Pass the working yarn in front of the first spoke and, with a yarn needle, short knitting needle, or your finger, lift the bottom loop over the yarn above it and drop it into the hole in the center of the spool. The top piece of working yarn has now become the bottom loop. Repeat with each spoke, always working in the

same direction. Shortly you will begin to see the cord coming out of the bottom of the spool. Continue until the cord is as long as you want it to be.

3 To remove the cord from the spool, transfer the last knitted stitch to the next spoke to be worked (this means that you remove the stitches in the same direction that you knitted them). Lift the bottom stitch over the top stitch. Repeat, always moving in the same direction, until you have 1 stitch left. Cut the end of the yarn so that you have a tail of about 5 inches and thread the tail onto a yarn needle. Carefully lift the last stitch from its spoke and thread the yarn through it. Pull tightly to secure.

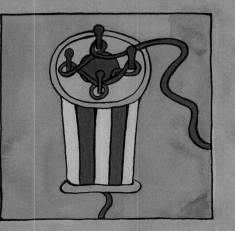
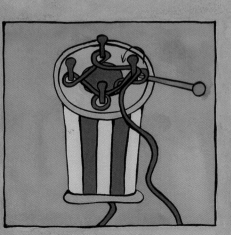

polka-dot & acorn-cap knitting needles

These colorful clay-topped and acorn-capped needles are so easy to make that you may want to whip up a few extra pairs as gifts for other knitters: They add a special touch to a handknit present if, for example, they're tucked into the folds of a scarf or tied up in the ribbons of the box's giftwrap. The needles take less than an hour from start to finish (just a bit longer if you count the time it takes for the glue to dry on the clay balls). Dowels can be bought at hardware or crafts stores. The more carefully you sand them, the smoother they will be and the better they will work for knitting. A ¼-inch dowel will make needles that are approximately size 10; A ³⁄₁₆-inch dowel will make needles that are approximately size 8. Any size dowel can be turned into a needle, but smaller ones tend to break and larger ones may feel uncomfortable in your hands when you are knitting. Ask an adult to help you cut the dowel and bake the polka-dot balls.

materials

· · · · · · · · · · ·

Wax paper

2 or more colors polymer clay, such as Fimo or Sculpey, or 2 acorn caps

¼-inch or ³⁄₁₆-inch dowel, cut into 2 approximately 10-inch-long pieces

Pencil sharpener

Fine-grit sandpaper

Lemon oil, mineral oil, or lavender oil

Craft glue

directions

to make the polka-dot balls

1. Prepare your work space by placing a piece of wax paper on a flat surface in a well-ventilated kitchen. Preheat the oven to the temperature specified on the label of your polymer clay (about 250° F).

2. Choose a main color of clay and soften it by warming it between your hands (this may take a few minutes, especially if the clay is old). Break off 2 pieces, each about ½ inch in diameter, and roll each piece between your hands into a smooth ball. Do not make the balls too large or they will weigh down the needles.

3. Break off tiny pieces (about 1/16 inch) of the second color of clay and form them into tiny balls. Press the tiny balls evenly onto the surface of the large balls, then roll the large balls to make them smooth and round again.

4. Press a ball onto 1 end of each dowel, then lay the dowels on top of a baking sheet so that the balls hang over the edge. Place in the oven, making sure that the balls do not touch the oven shelf. Bake according to the directions on the label of your clay until the balls have hardened (about 30 minutes). Set aside until cool enough to handle, about 10 minutes, then remove the balls from the dowels with a gentle tug (if they have not already fallen off).

to make the needles

1. Using the pencil sharpener, sharpen 1 end of each dowel until each tip is about as pointy as a dull pencil. Don't worry if the dowel becomes too pointy; you can make it dull again with sandpaper.

2. Rub each dowel with sandpaper until very smooth, making sure that each point is dull.

3. With a paper towel or clean rag, rub the dowels with oil until both are shiny and extra smooth.

4. Fill the hole in each polka-dot ball about ¼ of the way to the top with glue or squeeze a thin layer of glue into the inside of the acorn caps. Insert the flat end of each dowel into the balls or acorn caps. Wipe off any excess glue immediately. Set the needles aside in an empty glass or can, tips down, until dry, about 30 minutes.

where does yarn come from?

This picture shows plants and animals that give us natural fibers. Clockwise fron the top right corner, we have a cashmere goat (cashmere); an angora goat (mohair); an angora rabbit (angora); a sheep (wool); and an alpaca (alpaca). The words in parentheses are the names of the fibers that grow on these animals' bodies. Traveling up the right side of the illustration are silkworms (silk). On the left is a cotton plant (cotton). To find out how to see these animals or plants in person, check with a local yarn shop, 4-H club, veterinarian, pet store, or zoo. Yarn can also be made with chemicals. These are called synthetics, and acrylic is the most common synthetic used for knitting.

knitting with two needles

Get ready to learn the 3 most important skills in knitting: casting on, the knit stitch, and binding off. You'll need a pair of straight needles and a ball of yarn. Choose needles that feel good in your hands—they should be size 6 or larger and about 10 inches long. The yarn should be bulky or worsted-weight and wound into a ball. Depending on how long and wide you make your first piece of knitting, you can use it as a bookmark, a belt, a necktie, a small magic carpet, a doll's blanket—or you can make the bean bags shown on page 34. Have fun!

single cast-on
part one

Casting on is the process of placing your first row of stitches on 1 of your knitting needles. Two different cast-on methods are presented in this chapter: the single cast-on described here and the knit-on cast-on outlined on page 32. Most beginners find the single cast-on easier to learn first. The first step in casting on is making a slip knot.

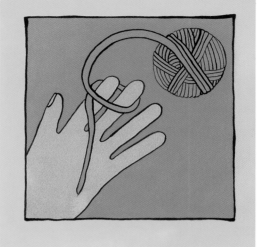

1 With your palm facing you, wrap the yarn around 2 of your fingers so that the working yarn (the yarn coming from the ball) crosses in front of the tail of the yarn.

2 With the fingers of your free hand, push the working yarn up through the loop formed on your fingers so that the working yarn forms a second loop.

3 Hold the second loop with 1 hand and pull down on the tail with the other to make a slip knot.

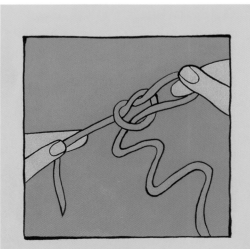

single cast-on
part two

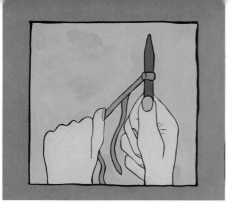

1 Slide the slip knot onto a knitting needle and tighten it enough to keep it from falling off (you should be able to move it with your fingers). Hold the needle with the slip knot in your right hand. Grab the working yarn with the fingers of your left hand, palm facing away from you.

2 Rotate your left wrist so that the working yarn wraps once around your thumb and the nails of the fingers holding the yarn are facing you.

3 Insert the tip of the needle in an upward direction through the center of the loop of yarn that has formed on your thumb.

4 Slide your thumb away so that a new stitch is added to the needle and pull the working yarn so that the new stitch is tight enough to stay on the needle if you turn the needle upside down but is still loose enough for you to move it with your fingers. Repeat steps 1 through 4 until you have the number of stitches you want on your needle. Include the slip knot when you are counting your stitches.

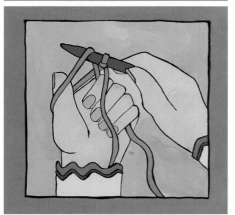

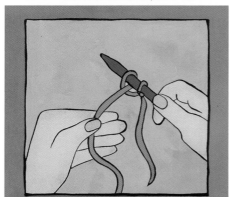

the knit stitch
completing your first row of knitting

The knit stitch is the stitch used to actually create fabric. To help you to remember each step, try reciting the poem on page 30 as you practice.

1 Hold the needle with the stitches on it in your left hand with your ball of yarn behind the needle. Hold the other needle in your right hand.

2 Insert the tip of the right needle up into the center of the top loop on the left needle so that the 2 needles cross each other to make an X shape and the right needle is in the back.

3 Hold the 2 needles in your right hand by placing your right thumb on top of the front needle and your right forefinger and middle finger underneath the needle in back so that your fingertips are holding (or pinching) the X shape.

4 Pick up the working yarn (the yarn connected to the ball) with your left hand and wrap it around the back needle from back to front to back, ending by gently lifting your right forefinger so that the yarn can be placed underneath it. Hold the yarn in place with your right forefinger. Note that the yarn starts in the back and finishes in the back.

5 Gently grasp the top needle with your left hand. Without letting go of the yarn under your right forefinger, insert the tip of the back needle (the needle in your right hand) down into the center of the stitch on the needle in your left hand, then toward your body.

6 Pull the needle in your right hand up so that the stitch on the needle in your left hand slides off the tip of the left needle. You now have 1 stitch on the right-hand needle. This is your first knit stitch. Repeat with the remaining stitches on the left-hand needle.

While you are working, carefully watch what you are doing and notice that the yarn wrapped around the needle in step 4 actually becomes the new stitch. When you finish, all of the stitches that started out on your left needle will have moved along with a new row of stitches to your right needle. Now place the needle with all of the stitches in your left hand (so that the end with the tail of yarn is on the right-hand side of the needle in your left hand) and start again at step 1. Continue until your piece of knitting is the length you want it to be, then bind off (page 33).

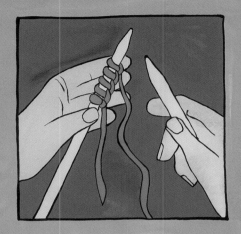

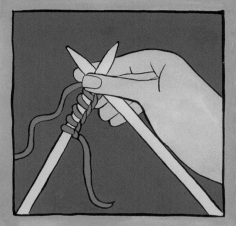
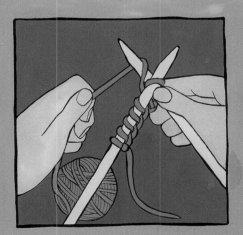
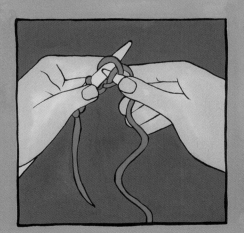
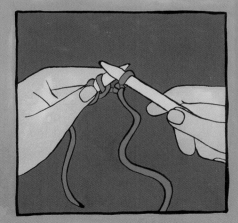

A Poem to Knit by

· · · · · · · · · · · · · · · ·

If you are having trouble remembering each step of the knit stitch, make up a poem to go with each movement. Here's an example:

Under the fence

(Insert the tip of the right needle up into the center of the top loop on the left needle.)

Catch the sheep

(Wrap the yarn from back to front around the right [back] needle.)

Back we come

(Insert the tip of the right needle down into the center of the stitch on the left needle, then toward your body.)

Off we leap

(Pull the right needle up so that the stitch on the left needle slides off the tip of left needle.)

keeping your knitting with you

One of the wonderful things about knitting is that you can take it with you wherever you go: in the car, to a friend's house, on a camping trip. All you need is a bag in which to carry your project. It should be made of a strong, tightly woven fabric, so that the tips of your needles cannot poke through it. For instructions on how to make your own tote bag, see page 51.

keeping track of your needles

When you knit, you are almost always moving stitches from the needle in your left hand to the needle in your right hand. Sometimes this can be difficult to remember. To make it easier, try one of the following tricks:

1 Use 2 different-colored needles—a pink one and a yellow one, for example. Each time you start a new row, remind yourself which way you are working, either yellow to pink or pink to yellow. This means you will need to have 2 sets of needles in the same size but in different colors. If you are learning to knit with a friend, you can buy a set of needles in one color and he or she can buy a set in a different color. Then you can trade so that you both have 1 needle in each color.

2 To make 2 identical needles look different, brush nail polish or paint onto the bottom end (the end with the knob) of one of them. Or wrap a piece of tape around the needle near the knob. Electrical tape is a good choice because it comes in different colors, such as red, green, or black, and will look nicer on your needle than ordinary adhesive tape.

knit-on Cast-on

Once you have mastered the knit stitch, it is easy to learn the knit-on cast-on. Use the single cast-on for your first few projects, then when you are feeling confident try this cast-on, which gives you a neater edge.

Make a slip knot, place the needle with the slip knot in your left hand, and follow steps 1 through 5 of the instructions for the knit stitch (page 28). Instead of lifting the stitch off the left needle (step 6), insert the left needle up into the center of the stitch on your right needle and transfer the stitch on your right needle to your left needle. Pull gently on the working yarn to tighten the new stitch a little, but do not make the stitch so tight that it won't slide on the needle. Repeat until you have casted on the number of stitches you need for your project.

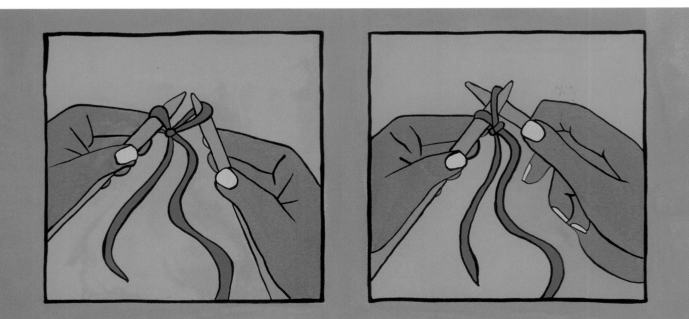

binding off

Binding off is the process of taking the last row of stitches off the knitting needles and securing the stitches so they will not unravel.

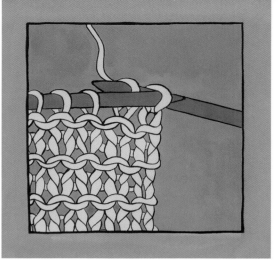

1 Starting at the beginning of a row, knit 2 stitches as usual. Insert your left needle down into the bottom stitch on the right needle. Gently hold the top stitch in place with your right forefinger and lift the bottom stitch over the top stitch and off the tip of the right needle. This is the same action used in finger knitting and spool knitting, but here you're using straight needles.

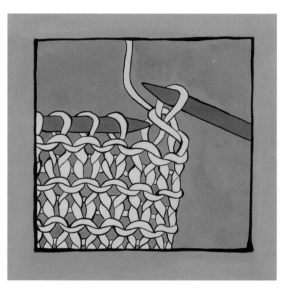

2 Slide the left needle away from the stitch. You now have 1 stitch on the right needle. Knit the next stitch from the left onto the right needle as usual. Repeat steps 1 and 2, never working with more than 2 stitches on your right needle. Continue until there is 1 stitch remaining on your right needle.

3 Cut the working yarn about 4 inches from the needle. Pull gently on your right needle to make the remaining stitch larger. Insert the end of the yarn through the stitch on the needle and remove the needle. Gently pull on the end of the yarn to tighten.

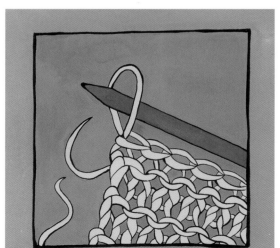

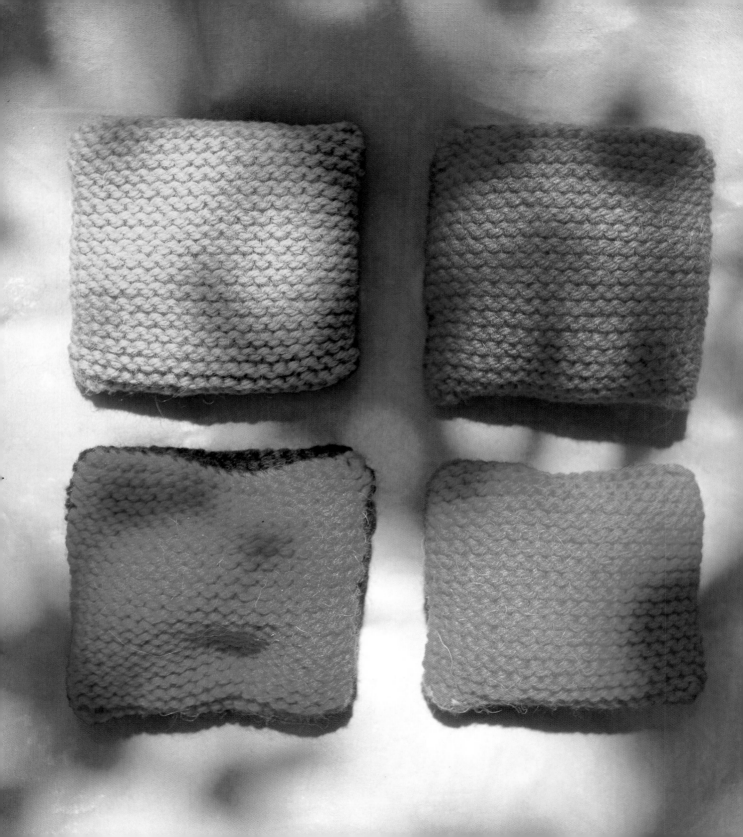

the basic bean bag

The Basic Bean Bag is the perfect project to begin with because it is easy to make and you only need a small amount of yarn. You can buy new yarn in your favorite color or you can use scrap yarn that is laying around the house. Basically, to make the bean bag, you cast on and repeat the knit stitch every row until you have made a square. After you have made 2 squares you sew them together and stuff them with dried beans. The technique of repeating the knit stitch over and over is known as garter stitch.

To check to see if you have made a square, try this simple trick: Lay your knitting (still on the needle) on a flat surface. Lift 1 of the bottom corners up to meet the opposite top corner. If the folded fabric forms 2 identical triangles on top of each other, congratulations! You have made a perfect square.

Make 3 or 4 bean bags and use them for juggling. Or make 1 bean bag and use it to play catch, as a paperweight or pincushion, or as a Hackey Sack. The 2 squares that make up the bean bags can be the same color or 2 different colors.

materials

. . . .

- **1 skein bulky yarn, such as Classic Elite Artisan**
- **1 pair size 8 knitting needles (or whatever size feels comfortable)**
- **About ¾ cup dried beans for each bean bag**
- **8-inch-long tube of thin nylon sock, tights, or pantyhose for each bean bag**
- **Yarn needle**

directions

1 Cast on 20 stitches. Work in garter stitch (knit every row) until you have a square. Bind off. Repeat so that you have 2 squares that are exactly the same size.

2 Using the yarn needle, sew the 2 squares together along 3 sides, following the instructions for either the mattress stitch or the overcast stitch (see right).

3 Make a very tight knot at 1 end of the length of sock, tights, or pantyhose to close it securely. If you are using the foot of the sock or tights, you can skip this step. Fill the tube with the beans. Place the tube inside the bean bag to see if you need to add or take away beans. The bean bag should be puffed like a pillow but the beans should not be bursting out. When you have the right amount of beans in the tube, close it by tying the extra fabric in a knot or by tying a piece of yarn around it. Make sure that the tube is very securely closed.

4 Using the yarn needle, sew the open side of the bean bag shut, following the instructions for either the mattress stitch or the overcast stitch.

What Size Are Your Bean Bags?

• • • • • • • • • • • • • • • •

Three factors are going to determine the size of your bean bags: the thickness of your yarn, the size of your needles, and how loosely or tightly you knit. (Everyone knits differently.) Take a look at your first bean bag. If the stitches look very loose and you would like them to be tighter, try using smaller needles. This will also make the overall size of your bean bag smaller. If the stitches are very tight and you would like them to be looser, try using larger needles. This will also make the overall size of your bean bag larger. The bean bags in the photo on page 34, which are about 5 inches square, were knit with size 8 needles.

sewing together the bean bags

When it's time to sew together your bean bags, you have 2 choices. You can use the mattress stitch or the overcast stitch. If you use the mattress stitch, the sewing yarn will be practically invisible. Make sure you sew the cast-on and bind-off edges of the first half to the cast-on and bind-off edges of the second half, working inside the ridges.

mattress stitch

Place the 2 halves of the bean bag next to each other with the sides you want to show on the outside facing you. Thread the yarn needle with the same yarn you used for knitting and stitch as shown below. After you have sewn together the first side, fold the 2 halves together (with the sides you want to show facing out) so that you have a single square shape. Continue to sew 2 more sides. Fill the bean bag, then sew up the 4th side.

overcast stitch

Place the 2 halves of the bean bag one on top of the other. Thread the yarn needle with the same yarn you used for knitting or yarn in a different color and sew together 3 sides as shown below. If you don't want your sewing yarn to show as much, sew the first 3 sides together, right sides facing in, then, just before filling with the beans, turn the bag right side out. Fill the bean bag, then sew up the 4th side.

pocket scarf & hat set

Part of the fun of knitting is playing with different colors of yarn. The scarf and hat at left were made with 5 colors of bulky wool yarn, but you can get a similar alternating effect with only 2 colors. Either use the color schemes shown here or create your own unique combination of colors. The following instructions are written for the 5-color version. If you stick to 2 colors, simply use the main color for the body of the scarf and the first half of the hat and the other color for the pockets on the scarf and the second half of the hat. Use either for the tassels. Sasha's set on page 43 was made with red and blue yarn.

materials

- To make the 5-color hat and scarf: approximately 280 yards gold and 70 yards each purple, pink, green, and teal bulky yarn, such as Tahki Cottage
- 1 pair size 10 knitting needles
- Yarn needle
- 1 piece of cardboard, approximately 5 inches square, to make tassels
- 5 safety pins

Taking Your Gauge

Once you have knit about 5 inches of the scarf or hat, lay a ruler over your work and count the number of stitches in a 4-inch-wide section. This is called taking the gauge (gauge rhymes with page). The gauge of the hat and scarf in the photograph is 15 stitches over 4 inches. Taking the gauge will become very important as you gain experience in knitting. Right now you're just doing it for practice.

to make the hat

1 To make the first half of the hat, cast on 34 stitches with the purple yarn. Work in garter stitch (knit every row) for approximately 9 inches. Bind off. Set aside this piece of knitting.

2 To make the second half of the hat, cast on 34 stitches with the green yarn. Work in garter stitch (knit every row) until this half of the hat is exactly the same size as the first half. Bind off.

3 Sew the 2 halves of the hat together using the yarn needle, pink yarn, and the overcast stitch: With the cast-on edges at the bottom, pin, then sew the purple piece to the green piece along 1 of the side edges. Sew the second side edge. If you have forgotten how to do the overcast stitch, see page 37.

4 Sew the top of the hat together, as follows: Fold the hat so the edges you just stitched run up the center front and the center back. With the yarn needle, teal yarn, and the overcast stitch, sew the top of the hat together.

5 Make 2 tassels using the gold yarn (see page 41 for detailed instructions). Attach the tassels to the 2 top corners of the hat. Weave in all of the loose ends, following the instructions at right.

Weaving in Ends

· · · · · · · · · · · · · · · · · ·

One way to make your knitting look neat is to hide any loose strands of yarn, such as the extra few inches of yarn at the cast-on edge and the bind-off edge. This is very easy to do. Thread the loose strand of yarn onto a yarn needle. Run the needle and yarn over and under the nearest stitches for about 2 inches, leaving a short (approximately 1-inch) tail of yarn showing on the back side of the work. Whenever possible, weave the ends of yarn into the edge of the knitting rather than into the center.

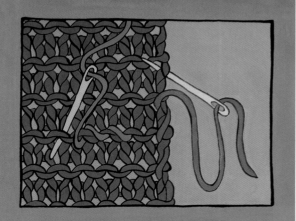

making tassels

1 Cut a piece of cardboard into a square so that each side is equal to the length you want the tassel to be. For example, if you want a 5-inch-long tassel, then you need to cut a 5-inch square. Wrap the yarn around the cardboard until it is as thick as you want. The more yarn you wrap the fatter your tassel will be.

Cut the end of the yarn, leaving a tail of about 15 inches, then run it under all of the wrapped yarn on 1 side of the cardboard and make a knot so that half of the wrapped yarn is on each side of the knot.

2 Remove the cardboard and cut the loops of yarn opposite the knot so that they become loose strands, then wrap the tail a few times around all of the yarn about an inch or so below the knot. Make a second knot so that the wrapping can't unravel.

Thread the tail onto a yarn needle and run the needle and yarn back into the knot at the top of the tassel. Use the leftover yarn to attach the tassel to your knitting.

to make the scarf

1 To make the body of the scarf, cast on 27 stitches with the gold yarn. Work in garter stitch (knit every row) for about 50 inches. Bind off all stitches. Cut the yarn so that there is a tail of about 6 inches attached to the scarf.

2 To make the first pocket, cast on 19 stitches with the pink yarn. Work in garter stitch (knit every row) for 6 inches. Bind off all stitches. Cut the yarn so that there is a tail of about 3 inches attached to the pocket.

3 To make the second pocket, cast on 19 stitches with the teal yarn. Work in garter stitch (knit every row) until the second pocket is exactly the same size as the first pocket. Cut the yarn so that there is a tail of about 3 inches attached to the pocket.

4 Weave in all of the gold ends of yarn attached to the scarf. (See page 40 if you do not know how to weave in the ends.) Measure 1 inch from 1 of the short edges of the scarf. Pin the pink pocket in place. With the yarn needle, green yarn, and the overcast stitch, neatly sew the bottom and side edges of the pocket to the scarf, tucking any extra tails of yarn inside the pocket. Measure 1 inch from the other short edge of the scarf. Pin the teal pocket in place. With the purple yarn, neatly sew the pocket in place, tucking any extra tails of yarn inside the pocket. Weave in the remaining loose ends.

Starting a New Ball of Yarn

· · · · · · · · · · · · · · · ·

It is time to attach a new ball of yarn when the one you started with is about to run out or when you want to change colors, such as when you are knitting stripes. Always try to start a new ball of yarn at the beginning of a row instead of in the middle of a row.

To start a new ball, cut the yarn you are replacing, leaving about a 4-inch tail. Loosely tie the new yarn around the old yarn with a knot and slide the knot so that it is as close as possible to the next stitch to be knit. Start knitting with the new yarn. When you are finished with your project, weave the tails of loose yarn into the side seams or edges.

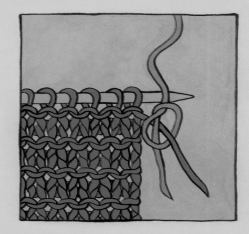

patchwork afghan

A bunch of bright garter-stitch squares are sewn together to create this patch-work afghan. You can use 2 colors, 10 colors, or even more—it's up to you. The size of the afghan is determined by how many squares you make and how big they are. You can knit a small afghan for a baby or a doll, or a big one to put on a bed—or on a llama, if, like Stanley at left, you just happen to have 1 on hand!

A large afghan requires a lot of work, so think about getting together with a bunch of friends or your brothers and sisters to knit one. Each of you can make a few squares, and then sew them all together. When you are done, why not present it as a group gift to someone special, such as a teacher or grandparent?

directions

materials

· · · · · · · · · · · ·

2 or more colors bulky yarn, such as Classic Elite Artisan

1 pair size 10 knitting needles (or whatever size feels comfortable)

Yarn needle

Pencil and paper

1 To make an approximately 12-inch square, cast on 36 stitches. To make an approximately 6-inch square, cast on 18 stitches. Work in garter stitch (knit every row) until you have made a square. The length and width should be the same. Check by measuring with a ruler or tape measure or by using the method described on page 35.

2 Make 6, 9, or 12 squares, depending on how large you want your afghan to be. After you have knit 1 square, count the number of stitches in a 4-inch-wide section. This is

called taking your gauge. The gauge of the afghans in the photographs is 12 stitches over 4 inches (or 3 stitches per inch). It is not important that your gauge is the same for this project (since the afghan does not need to be a specific size). But, later on, taking your gauge will become very important, so it's a good idea to start practicing now.

3 Lay all of the squares out on the floor and move them around until you like the way the different colors look next to each other. Using the pencil and paper, draw a small map to show where each square will go.

4 Thread a double strand of yarn through the yarn needle and begin sewing together the squares using the overcast stitch (page 37). To keep the afghan from stretching out too much, always sew the cast-on or bind-off edge of 1 square to the side edge of another square. Sew together the squares in rows, then sew the rows to each other. For example, if you are making a 12-square afghan, sew 3 squares at a time to make 4 separate rows, then sew the 4 rows together.

5 Thread the yarn needle with a long strand of yarn and decorate all the seams with a large, slanted sewing stitch.

Knitting to Show You Care

Sharing what you knit with your friends and family makes you feel good. Knitting for someone you don't know well may make you feel even better, especially if that someone needs a little bit of extra care, such as a person who has lost his or her home or is ill. Think about knitting something, such as a hat, a doll, or a blanket, for the kids or grown-ups in a homeless shelter or for babies who are sick and in the hospital. Receiving a handmade gift can often make people who are sad feel more hopeful. You can give your handknits away in the town where you live or you can be part of a national effort, such as Caps for Kids or Warm Up America! These 2 organizations collect and distribute handknits to people who need them. Write to the Craft Yarn Council of America for guidelines on how these 2 programs work:

Craft Yarn Council of America (CYCA)
2500 Lowell Road, Gastonia, NC 28054

CHAPTER THREE

Shaping

Up to this point, everything you have knit has been either a square or a rectangle. Now it's time to learn how to make different shapes. This is done by "increasing" or "decreasing"—knitting terms for adding or taking away stitches. To increase the size of your fabric you add stitches. To decrease its size you take stitches away. Increasing and decreasing are used to shape the Garter Stitch Dolls and the ears of the Owl & Pussycat Bath Puppets in this chapter. They are also used for shaping the sleeves of sweaters and rounding the toes of socks. To find out what Sasha and Emily are doing in the photo, see Sheep to Shawl on page 64.

increasing

There are a few different ways to increase. The easiest is to simply cast on extra stitches using the single cast-on method on page 26. Simply follow the instructions from the point after you have made the slip knot.

Another way to increase is to knit into the same stitch twice, as follows:

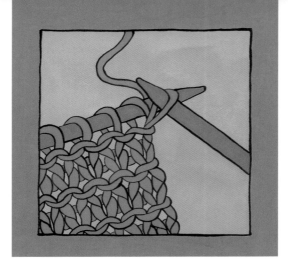

1 Knit into the top stitch on your left needle as usual but don't lift this stitch off the left needle (you are completing steps 1 through 5 on page 28).

2 Insert the tip of your right needle down into the center of the top stitch on your left needle and knit it again, but this time lift it off the left needle. You should now have 2 more stitches on your right needle.

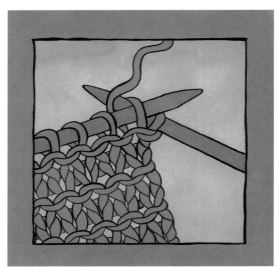

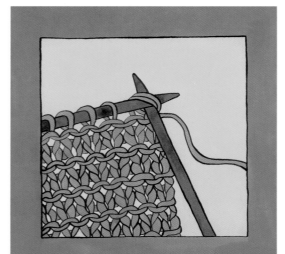

decreasing

The easiest way to decrease is to knit 2 stitches together. Insert your right needle into the 2 top stitches on your left needle at the same time and knit as if you are working on 1 stitch.

kids knitting tote bag

Use this easy-to-make bag to carry around your latest knitting project. Make sure the fabric you choose is strong and tightly woven so that your needles can't poke through it.

1 Fold a 20-x-20-inch piece of strong, tightly woven cotton in half, right sides together, so the fold is on the left. Pin 1 short and 1 long side. Starting from the top right, sew 1 inch down, ½ inch in from the edge, using the back stitch and a sewing needle and thread. Make your stitches very small and even. Secure the last stitch with a knot. Leave 1 inch open (unsewn), then start sewing again until you reach ½ inch from the bottom. Turn the corner and sew to the fold. Secure the last stitch with a knot.

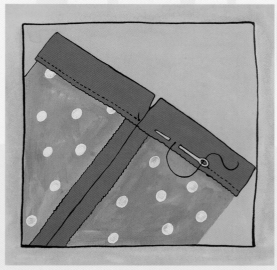

2 With an iron, press open the long seam. Fold the top of the bag down 2½ inches. Stitch the folded fabric in place close to the edge.

3 Turn the bag right side out. Attach a safety pin to 1 end of a 36-inch-long, ½-inch-wide piece of ribbon or knitted cord. Push the safety pin in 1 of the holes, all the way around, and out the other hole. Remove the safety pin and tie the 2 ends of the ribbon together in a knot. Pull the ribbon to shut the bag.

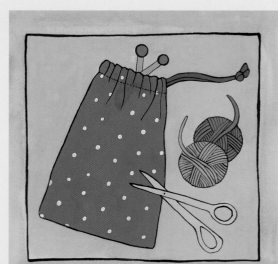

garter stitch dolls

These cute little dolls are transformed into different characters by changing the color of the yarn and a few simple features, such as the ears, eyes, or nose. The bear, gingerbread person, and curly-haired doll at left were knit with size 8 needles and bulky yarn. The vest the curly-haired doll is wearing can also be knit for any other approximately 15-inch-tall doll or stuffed animal you have at home.

materials

• • • • • • • • • • •

Approximately 175 yards bulky yarn, such as Schoolhouse Press Highland Wool, for 1 doll

Approximately 85 yards bulky yarn in a contrasting color, for vest

Scrap yarn, for making hair and embroidering features on the face

1 pair 14-inch-long size 8 knitting needles

Stitch holder or large safety pin

Yarn needle

Point protector or rubber band, if making curly hair

A few handfuls of unspun wool or synthetic fiber stuffing

Assorted buttons (for eyes, vest, and body of gingerbread person)

Sewing needle and thread

For this project, needles that are a little longer than 10 inches will work best because when you are knitting the section of the body that includes the arms, you will have 44 stitches on your needles, and if you knit the vest you'll be working with 52 stitches. Although 44 or 52 stitches will fit on a 10-inch needle, those near the end may fall off if you are not careful. Avoid the problem completely by starting out with needles that are about 14 inches long.

directions

to make the doll

1 **Make the first leg:** Cast on 10 stitches. Work in garter stitch (knit every row) until the leg measures about 5 inches. Cut the yarn, leaving a tail that is a few inches long. Slide the 10 stitches off the knitting needle and onto a stitch holder or safety pin.

2 **Make the second leg:** Cast on 10 stitches. Work in garter stitch (knit every row) until the second leg is exactly the same size as the first leg. Do not cut the yarn or remove the stitches from the needle.

3 **Make the lower body:** Knit the 10 stitches from the second leg. Knit the 10 stitches from the first leg (starting with the stitch connected to the tail of yarn) from the stitch holder onto the needle with the stitches for the second leg. You should now have 20 stitches on your needle and the tail of yarn from the first leg should be hanging down from the center. Work in garter stitch (knit every row) until the body measures about 4 inches from the point where you joined the 2 legs.

4 **Make the upper body and arms:** At the edge of the work, cast on 12 stitches for the first arm. Knit across all 32 stitches. Cast on another 12 stitches for the second arm. You should now have 44 stitches. Work in garter stitch (knit every row) until the arms measure about 2½ inches. At the beginning of the next row, bind off 17 stitches so that you have 27 stitches left on the needle. Knit to the end of the row. At the beginning of the next row, bind off 17 more stitches so that you have 10 stitches left on the needle. Knit to the end of the row.

5 **Make the head:** Work in garter stitch (knit every row) for 8 rows, increasing 1 stitch at the beginning of each row so that you end up with 18 stitches on the needle. (To increase, you cast on extra stitches— see page 50.) Work in garter stitch (knit every row) for 12 rows. Knit 8 more rows, decreasing 1 stitch at the beginning of each row so that you end up with 10 stitches on the needle. (To decrease, you knit 2 stitches together—see page 50.) Bind off.

6 **Make the second side:** Repeat steps 1 through 5 to make the second side of the doll. If you want, sew on button eyes and embroider on a nose and mouth. If you are making the gingerbread person, sew 3 buttons down the front of the body.

7 **Take your gauge:** Before sewing your doll together, take your gauge by measuring with a ruler the number of stitches in a 4-inch-wide section of the body. The gauge of the dolls in the photograph is 16 stitches over 4 inches (or 4 stitches to the inch). It is not important that your gauge is the same (since the dolls do not need to be a specific size). But, later on, taking your gauge will become very important, so it's a good idea to start practicing now.

Sewing on Buttons

Thread a needle narrow enough to fit through the holes in your buttons with about 10 inches of yarn or sewing thread. Make 2 small stitches at the spot on your knitting where you want to place the button. This will secure the yarn to the fabric. Poke the needle with the yarn up through 1 of the holes of the button (from the bottom of the button to the top), then down into the adjacent hole and through the knitted fabric. Now poke the tip of the needle up through the knitted fabric and into the first hole again. Do this 4 or 5 times. If the button has 4 holes, repeat with the 2 remaining holes. To secure, make several small stitches on the wrong side of the fabric, then run the needle and yarn under these stitches as well as a few stitches on the inside of the knitted fabric so that the yarn is hidden. Cut any leftover yarn with scissors.

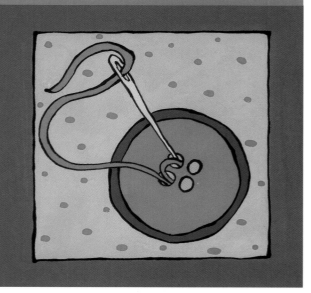

8 Sew and stuff: Thread the yarn needle with the same yarn you used to knit the doll and sew the doll together, leaving the top of the head open for stuffing. If you have forgotten how to sew together pieces of knitting, see page 37. Stuff the doll, then sew the top of the doll closed. You can decorate the doll with overcast stitching (see page 37) in a contrasting color, or add any optional features you like, such as bunny or bear ears or curly hair.

to make the optional features

curly hair: Cast on 20 stitches with whatever yarn you want to use for hair (wool will hold curls better than other fibers). Work in garter stitch (knit every row) for about 4 inches. Do not bind off. Place a point protector or a rubber band at the end of the needle holding your knitting so the stitches

Unusual Yarns

Believe it or not, you can knit with materials other than yarn. Finding nontraditional materials to knit with can be interesting detective work. For example, the garter stitch doll can be knit in wool, with string, or with raffia, which is a ribbonlike grass that is sold by florists and at arts and crafts stores and that was used to make the bunny below. Some people even knit with wire, although they often have to use pliers to bend it into the correct position, and this can be hard on the hands! Next time you're in a hardware or arts and crafts store, check out all the different kinds of string, twine, and plastic tapes and try to figure out which ones would work best for knitting.

do not fall off. Wet your piece of knitting completely, gently squeeze out the water, and set it aside to dry. When dry, unravel the knitting so that you have a long strand of curly yarn. Cut the yarn into pieces that are twice as long as you want the hair to be. To attach a length of hair to the doll, fold a piece in half, then with your fingers push the folded end through a stitch on the doll's head so you have a loop that is about an inch long coming out of the doll's head. Next insert the other 2 ends of the same length of hair through the loop and pull to tighten. Repeat with the rest of the hair. Trim the hair into a style you like.

bear ears: Cast on 8 stitches. Work in garter stitch (knit every row) for 4 rows. Cut the yarn so that you have a tail of about 8 inches. Thread the tail through a yarn needle, then through the stitches on the needle so that the stitches are held on the yarn. Pull the end of the yarn to make a half circle. Sew the ear onto 1 side of the head of the doll using what remains of the tail threaded through the yarn needle. Repeat for a second ear.

bunny ears: Cast on 12 stitches with 2 strands of yarn instead of 1. The easiest way to do this is to take yarn from 2 balls at the same time. If you do not already have 2 balls that are the same color, divide the yarn from 1 ball into 2. Work in garter stitch (knit every row) for 6 rows. Bind off. Sew the short end onto 1 side of the top of the head of the doll. Repeat for a second ear.

embroidery stitches

Embroidery is a lot like coloring, except you do it with yarn instead of crayons. It's a fun way to decorate pieces of knitting. Choose a smooth yarn that will show up well on top of the knitting—yarn that is too thin will disappear into the knitted stitches and yarn that is too thick will overpower them. A thin yarn can be doubled by threading it onto a yarn needle and pulling on the 2 ends so that they are the same length.

back stitch works well for straight or curved lines, such as a doll's mouth. **satin stitch** is a good choice when you are trying to fill in a space, such as the nose on a doll, with color. To learn these 2 stitches, follow the illustrations below. Be careful not to pull the embroidery stitches too tightly, or the knitted fabric will bunch up. If you make a mistake, gently pull out the stitches 1 by 1 and try again. It is a good idea to practice these embroidery stitches on pieces of paper or thin cardboard before you start to embroider on your knitting.

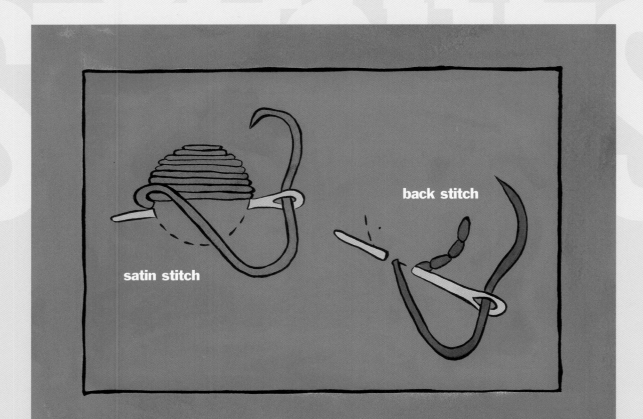

satin stitch

back stitch

to make the vest

If you want the vest to be oversized, so that it looks like a dress (as shown on the curly-haired doll), knit it using needles that are 1 or 2 sizes larger than the needles used to knit the doll. For example, if you knit the doll with size 8 needles, then knit the vest with size 10 needles. When you make the buttonholes for the vest, you will learn a new technique called the yarnover (see right).

The instructions for this vest are written in a different style than the instructions for the doll. Simply follow them row by row and you should not have any problems. To keep track of what you are doing, on a piece of paper write down the number of each row as you finish it.

for the lower body

Rows 1–8: Cast on 52 stitches, then work 8 rows in garter stitch (knit every row).

Row 9: Knit 2 stitches, then decrease 1 by knitting the next 2 stitches together. Make a yarnover, then knit to the end of the row.

Rows 10–16: Work these 7 rows in garter stitch.

Row 17: Knit 2 stitches, then decrease 1 by knitting the next 2 stitches together. Make a yarnover, then knit to the end of the row.

Rows 18–24: Work these 7 rows in garter stitch.

Row 25: Knit 2 stitches, then decrease 1 by knitting the next 2 stitches together. Make a yarnover, then knit to the end of the row.

for the left front

Rows 26–27: Knit 15 stitches, then place the remaining 37 stitches on the stitch holder (or the safety pin or a shoelace or scrap piece of yarn tied to hold the stitches in place). Turn the work around so that the opposite side is facing you. Now the needle with the stitches on it should be in your left hand and the working yarn should be attached to the top stitch. Let the 37 stitches on the holder hang to the side and knit the 15 stitches on the needle.

Row 28: Decrease 1 by knitting 2 stitches together, then knit to the end of the row.

Row 29: Knit to the end of the row.

Repeat rows 28 and 29 until there are 4 stitches remaining for the shoulder. Bind off.

for the back

Slip the middle 22 stitches on the holder from left to right onto a needle. These are the 22 stitches next to the left front (the remaining 15 stitches will be knit later to make the right front). Work 23 rows in garter stitch. Bind off. You will need to start the back section with a new piece of yarn. To do this, insert the right needle into the first stitch on the left needle as usual, then wrap the new yarn around the right needle, holding both ends—the tail and the end connected to the working yarn—securely with the fingers of your right hand, and pull the new stitch through as usual with your right needle. Continue to knit with the working yarn.

for the right front

Slip the remaining 15 stitches onto the needle from left to right. Remember that the 4th stitch on the holder is a yarnover; be careful that you do not let it fall off.

Row 26: Attach a new piece of yarn as you did for the back and knit to the end of the row.

Row 27: Decrease by knitting 2 stitches together, then knit to the end of the row.

Row 28: Knit to the end of the row.

Repeat rows 27 and 28 until there are 4 stitches remaining for the shoulder. Bind off.

finishing

Sew the shoulder seams together using the mattress stitch (see page 37). Sew 3 buttons opposite the 3 buttonholes (see page 55).

Yarnovers

· · · · · · · · · · · · · ·

A yarnover is a special way of increasing 1 stitch and at the same time making an intentional hole in your work. Yarnovers are used often when knitting lace (which is made up of lots of different-sized holes). They are also used in combination with a decrease to make an easy buttonhole, as in the doll's vest shown on pages 52 and 58.

Knit as usual until it is time to make the yarnover. When you are ready to make the yarnover, wrap the yarn once from front to back around the right needle. Knit the remaining stitches on the left needle as usual. The wrapped yarn becomes a new stitch. On the next row be careful not to let your new stitch fall off the needle: Make sure you knit it.

owl & pussycat bath puppets

These cotton puppets serve double duty. They become talented actors and actresses when you slip them onto your hands, then work perfectly as washcloths when you take them in the bath. Have you ever thought about putting on a puppet show in the tub?

The puppets shown here were made with 5 different colors of soft bulky cotton yarn. By changing needle size, you can make the puppets skinny or fat. The narrower puppets in the photograph were made with size 8 needles, the wider ones with size 10 needles. The eyes, noses, and mouths were made with buttons and embroidery. If you use the puppets in the bath, be sure to turn them around so that the buttons are on the top side of your hand. That way they won't scratch your skin while you scrub. Or, if you want, make eyes out of felt instead of buttons and sew them onto the puppets.

materials

. . . .

Approximately 60 yards bulky cotton yarn, such as Classic Elite Sand Cotton, for 1 puppet

Smooth scrap yarn for embroidering the nose and mouth and sewing together the puppet

1 pair size 8 or 10 knitting needles (or whatever size feels comfortable)

2 buttons for each puppet, for eyes

Sewing needle and thread

Yarn needle

directions

to make the pussycat

for the body

1 Cast on 42 stitches. Work in garter stitch (knit every row) until the piece measures about 4 inches.

2 In the next row, knit the first 28 stitches. Thread the yarn needle with scrap yarn in a different color and thread the last 14 stitches onto the yarn. Remove the needle and tie the ends of the yarn in a knot so that the stitches are held in place. These stitches will be knit again later to make the thumb.

3 Continue working the 28 stitches in garter stitch (knit every row) until the piece measures about 7½ or 8 inches. Bind off all 28 stitches.

4 Untie the yarn that is holding the 14 thumb stitches in place and slip those stitches back onto the knitting needle. Remove the scrap yarn. Work the 14 stitches in garter stitch (knit every row) until the thumb measures about 6 or 6½ inches. Bind off all 14 stitches. You will need to start the thumb with a new piece of yarn. To do this, insert the right needle into the first stitch on the left needle as usual, then wrap the new yarn around the right needle, holding both ends—the tail and the end connected to the working yarn— securely with the fingers of your right hand, and pull the new stitch through as usual with your right needle. Continue to knit with the working yarn.

5 Take your gauge by measuring with a ruler the number of stitches in a 4-inch-wide section. The gauge of the puppets in the photograph ranges from 14 to 16 stitches over 4 inches (3½ to 4 stitches per inch). It is not important that your gauge be the same for this project (since the puppets do not need to be a specific size), but it is important that you know how to do this for future projects.

6 Fold the thumb stitches in half so that the 2 side edges meet each other. Using the yarn needle, smooth scrap yarn, and the overcast stitch (see page 37), sew the thumb together starting at the top and continuing until you reach the point where the thumb meets the hand. Now fold the other side for the hand in to meet the thumb section. Sew from the bottom cast-on edge to connect the thumb and the rest of the hand section. Continue sewing around from the point where the thumb meets the hand up and around the hand section. Turn the puppet right side out. (The inside of the puppet has now become the outside and you don't have to worry that the yarn used for sewing the puppet together will show.) Weave in any loose ends of yarn.

for the ears

1 **Rows 1–3:** Cast on 7 stitches, leaving a tail of yarn that measures about 6 inches when you make the slip knot. Work in garter stitch (knit every row) for 3 rows.

Row 4: Knit 5 stitches. Decrease 1 by knitting the last 2 stitches together. You now have 6 stitches on your needle.

Row 5: Knit 4 stitches. Decrease 1 by knitting the last 2 stitches together. You now have 5 stitches on your needle.

Row 6: Knit 3 stitches. Decrease 1 by knitting the last 2 stitches together. You now have 4 stitches on your needle.

Row 7: Knit 2 stitches. Decrease 1 by knitting the last 2 stitches together. You now have 3 stitches on your needle.

Row 8: Knit 1 stitch. Decrease 1 by knitting the last 2 stitches together. You now have 2 stitches on your needle.

Row 9: Knit 2 stitches together. You now have 1 stitch on your needle.

Cut the yarn and pull the tail through the last stitch. Repeat to make a second ear.

2 Using the yarn needle and the tail of yarn at the cast-on edge of each ear, sew the ears to the top of the puppet.

finishing

With a sewing needle and thread, sew on the button eyes (see page 55 if you don't know how to sew on the buttons). Embroider on a nose in a triangle or diamond shape. Using a different color of yarn, embroider the mouth (see page 57 if you don't know how to embroider).

to make the owl

1 Cast on 36 stitches. Work in garter stitch (knit every row) until the piece measures about 7½ or 8 inches. Bind off all stitches.

2 Fold the piece of knitting in half with the cast-on edge at the bottom. Sew the open side and top closed using the yarn needle, smooth scrap yarn, and the overcast stitch (see page 37). Turn the puppet right side out. (The inside of the puppet has now become the outside and you don't have to worry that the yarn used for sewing the puppet together will show.) Weave in any loose ends of yarn.

3 Make the ears and sew them onto the owl body, following the instructions for the pussycat puppet. Sew on button eyes and embroider the face, following the instructions for the pussycat puppet.

sheep to shawl

The wool that you see on a sheep goes through a lot to become the wool that you buy in a store. Although modern machines can do some of this work very quickly, many people still like to create yarn at home, following the steps shown here. These methods have been in use for hundreds of years.

1 shearing The fiber (or fleece) is removed from the sheep, usually with a type of electric scissors called shears. The shearer removes most of the fleece in 1 piece. It is then skirted, which means the really dirty parts are thrown away. The fiber that grows on sheep is called wool.

2 grading A grader judges different sections of the fleece, such as the back, belly, and legs, by looking at many of its characteristics, including its length, fineness, and strength, because quality of wool can vary. He or she then separates the wool into piles according to its quality.

3 washing Next, the wool is washed to remove anything that is not supposed to be in it, such as pieces of grass, hay, or manure.

4 carding To untangle the fibers so that they are all lined up in 1 direction, the wool is combed with paddles called carders. This process is called carding. (It's what Sasha and Emily are doing in the photo at the beginning of this chapter.)

5 spinning The carded fibers are then pulled apart, overlapped, and twisted together on a spindle or spinning wheel to create 1 long piece of yarn. The yarn is taken off the spindle or spinning wheel and wound into skeins (rhymes with rains).

6 dyeing Depending on the individual sheep from which the wool came, the color of the yarn can range from creamy white to dark brown. Sometimes the yarn is dyed with either natural dyes (usually made from plants) or chemical dyes. Finally, the yarn is wound into a ball. It is now ready for knitting.

Sometimes at special sheep festivals, people take part in Sheep to Shawl Contests, working in teams to complete all of the above steps and knit a shawl in 1 day. The team that does the best job wins.

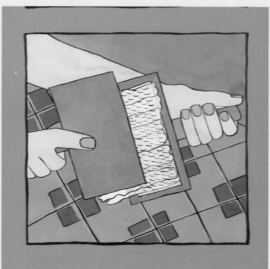

the purl stitch, stockinette stitch, and ribbing

There's more to knitting than the knit stitch! Most of the projects up to this point, from the bean bags to the bath puppets, have been made using this stitch. Now it's time to introduce the purl stitch. The knit stitch and the purl stitch are actually the reverse of each other— the front of the purl stitch looks like the back of the knit stitch and vice versa. When you cast on and purl all your stitches the result will not look any different than the knit stitch. But when you combine the knit stitch and the purl stitch in different ways, exciting things happen.

the purl stitch

Purling takes practice, but if you already know the knit stitch, it's a cinch to learn. When you combine the knit and purl stitches in different ways, you can create bumpy or stretchy fabric.

1 Hold the needle with the stitches on it in your left hand and the ball of yarn in front of your needles. Hold the other needle in your right hand.

2 Insert the tip of the right needle down into the center of the top stitch on the left needle so that the right needle crosses in front of the left needle.

3 Hold the 2 needles in your right hand by placing your right thumb on top of the front needle and your right forefinger underneath the needle in back so that your fingertips are holding both needles in place.

4 Pick up the working yarn (the yarn coming from the ball) with your left hand and wrap it around the front needle from front to back to front, ending by gently lifting your right thumb so that the yarn can be placed underneath it. Hold the yarn in place with your right thumb. (Note that the yarn both starts and finishes in the front.)

5 Gently grasp the left needle with your left hand. Without letting go of the yarn under your right thumb, slide the tip of the front needle (the needle in your right hand) backward (away from your body) and up into the center of the stitch on the left needle.

6 Pull the right needle up so that the stitch on the left needle slides off the tip of the left needle. You have completed your first purl stitch. Repeat for the remaining stitches on your left needle. While you are working, watch what you are doing carefully and notice that the yarn looped around the needle in step 4 actually becomes the new stitch. When you finish, all the stitches that started out on your left needle will have moved along with a new row of stitches to your right needle. Now place the needle with all the stitches in your left hand and start again at step 1. Continue until your piece of knitting is the length you want it to be, then bind off.

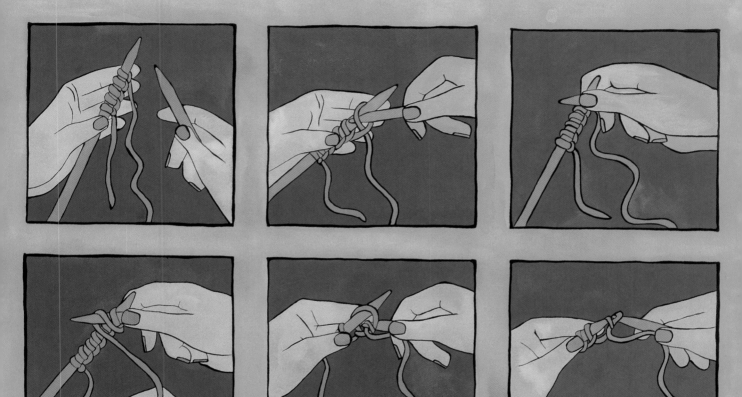

four bean bags

Once you get the hang of the purl stitch, you can combine it with the knit stitch to create all sorts of fabric. In the process of practicing the 2 stitches together, make these alternatives to the Basic Bean Bags on page 34. Like them, these 4 were knit with bulky yarn and size 8 needles.

purl (or garter stitch) bean bags

These bean bags will look exactly like the Basic Bean Bags on page 34. Either could also be called Garter Stitch Bean Bags, because when you do the knit stitch in every row or the purl stitch in every row, the result is the same: It is called garter stitch.

Cast on 20 stitches. Purl every row until you have a square. Bind off. Repeat so that you have 2 squares that are exactly the same size. To sew together and stuff, follow the instructions on page 36.

stockinette and reverse stockinette bean bags

The Stockinette and Reverse Stockinette Bean Bags are smaller than the Garter Stitch Bean Bag even though they are made with the same number of stitches because garter stitch naturally spreads from side to side more than stockinette stitch. As a result, you need to knit more rows in garter stitch to make a square than you need to knit in stockinette stitch.

If you knit odd rows and purl even rows, you end up with a fabric that is smooth on 1 side (called stockinette stitch) and bumpy on the other (called reverse stockinette stitch). Stockinette stitch is the most popular stitch in knitting. It's used to make lots of sweaters, smooth side out. The smooth side of stockinette stitch is called the front, the knit side, or the right side. The bumpy side is called the back, the purl side, or the wrong side.

Pieces of fabric made with stockinette and reverse stockinette stitches curl at the edges. The curl is controlled when you sew the pieces together. If you sew the squares together so that the smooth (knit) sides of the squares are facing out, you have a stockinette bean bag. If you sew the squares together so that the bumpy (purl) sides are facing out, you have a reverse stockinette bean bag.

Cast on 20 stitches.
Row 1: Knit all the way across.
Row 2: Purl all the way across.
Repeat rows 1 and 2 until you have a square. Make a second square that is exactly the same size. To sew together and stuff, follow the instructions on page 36.

ribbed bean bags

Because ribbing pulls in like elastic, the ribbed bean bag is the smallest of all. By alternating knit and purl stitches within each row, you create a stretchy fabric. Ribbing is used to help clothes fit well. You probably have a hat with ribbing at the bottom edge, or gloves with ribbing around the wrists.

It is really important that you are able to see the difference between knit stitches and purl stitches when you are ribbing. The knit stitches are the

purl (or garter) stitch

stockinette stitch

reverse stockinette stitch

ribbing

flat ones. The purl stitches are the bumpy ones. It will be easier to see the difference in the beginning if you choose a light color of yarn.

Cast on 20 or more stitches, making sure to cast on an even number of stitches. And remember: When you switch from doing a knit stitch to doing a purl stitch, you must move the working yarn from the back to the front of your needles. When you switch from doing a

purl stitch to a knit stitch, you must move the working yarn from the front to the back of your needles.
Row 1: Knit 1, purl 1. Repeat until you reach the end of the row.
Repeat row 1, knitting the knit stitches and purling the purl stitches, until you have a square. Make a second square that is exactly the same size. To sew together and stuff, follow the instructions on page 36.

crazy caterpillar

This cuddly Crazy Caterpillar is made with 4 colors of bulky yarn—black, green, blue, and pink. You will only need about 35 yards of each color to make a caterpillar like the one in the photograph, which is 14 inches long. Since 1 skein of yarn includes much more than that, split what you buy with a friend, or plan to have leftovers for another project. If you already have enough scrap yarn around the house, make the caterpillar with that. Then plop it atop your head for everyone to see, as did the lovely model on page 66 (her name is Molly).

materials

. . . .

Approximately 35 yards each of 4 colors bulky yarn, such as Classic Elite Artisan

1 pair size 8 needles (or whatever size feels comfortable)

Yarn needle

A few handfuls of beans, unspun wool, or synthetic fiber stuffing, for stuffing caterpillar

A tube of thin nylon sock, tights, or pantyhose (if using beans as stuffing), 6 inches longer than the finished length of your caterpillar

2 buttons

Sewing needle and thread

Small piece of felt, for eyelashes (optional)

The main stitch pattern used here—purl 1 row, knit 1 row, repeat—is reverse stockinette stitch. It's basically the same as stockinette stitch except that the bumpy side is facing out instead of the smooth side.

The buttons on the Crazy Caterpillar were made in Nepal, a country in Asia, and came from One World Button Supply Company, a small business in New York City that sells buttons crafted by artisans all over the world.

directions

to make the tail and body

1 With your first color of yarn, cast on 6 stitches. Purl 1 row. Knit 1 row, increasing by knitting into each stitch twice so that you end up with a total of 12 stitches (if you have forgotten how to increase using this method, see page 50). Purl 1 row. Knit the next row, increasing by knitting into each stitch twice so that you end up with a total of 24 stitches. Purl 1 row. Knit 1 row, increasing 1 stitch in every 4th stitch so that you end up with a total of 30 stitches.

2 Work in reverse stockinette stitch (purl 1 row, knit 1 row, repeat) for about 4½ inches, stopping after you have completed a knit row.

3 Join a second color of yarn. Work in standard stockinette stitch (knit 1 row, purl 1 row, repeat) for 6 rows, stopping after you have completed a purl row.

4 Join the third color of yarn. Knit 2 rows, then repeat step 2.

5 Repeat step 3, then join the fourth color of yarn. Knit 2 rows. Repeat step 2 except this time stop after you have completed a purl row.

to shape the head

Row 1: Still working with the fourth color of yarn, knit 3, then decrease 1 stitch by knitting 2 together, and repeat to the end of the row. When you finish the row you will have 24 stitches on your needle.

Row 2: Purl to the end of the row.

Row 3: Decrease by knitting 2 stitches together and repeat to the end of the row. When you finish you will have 12 stitches on your needle.

Row 4: Purl to the end of the row.

Row 5: Decrease 1 stitch by knitting 2 stitches together and repeat to the end of the row. When you finish you will have 6 stitches on your needle.

Row 6: Purl to the end of the row. Cut the yarn, leaving a tail that is about twice as long as your caterpillar. Thread the tail through the yarn needle, then insert the yarn needle and tail through the stitches on the knitting needle and pull to gather the stitches together. Using the tail of yarn, sew the back seam of the caterpillar, matching all of the colors on each side of the seam and leaving an opening at the tail end for stuffing the caterpillar. If you are using beans, tie a secure knot at 1 end of the sock, tights, or pantyhose (the knot is not necessary if you are using the foot). Fill with beans and tie tightly to keep them inside. Stuff the caterpillar with the bag of beans, or with unspun wool or synthetic fiber stuffing, and sew the opening shut. If you want, cut 2 star shapes out of the felt for eyelashes. Using the sewing needle and thread, attach the eyelashes and the 2 buttons for eyes.

three different looks: garter, stockinette, and ribbing

In these illustrations you can clearly see the differences among **garter stitch** (knit all stitches), **stockinette stitch** (knit every stitch in 1 row, purl every stitch in 1 row, repeat), and **ribbing** (knit 1 stitch, purl 1 stitch, repeat). The stitches and rows are numbered so that you can see where each stitch and row begins and ends. Study these illustrations, then look at your own work. Take some time to count each stitch, 1 by 1, and to count each row. The sooner you are able to see the differences, the quicker you will advance as a knitter.

garter stitch

stockinette stitch

ribbing

Wraparound ribbed scarf

This scarf is mighty long. Shown here in 3-Strand Merino Silver yarn from Morehouse Farm, it features a 3 x 3 rib, which means that the rib is made up of 3 knit stitches and 3 purl stitches. (A 2 x 2 rib is made up of 2 knit stitches and 2 purl stitches, and so on.) Merino sheep are a very special breed raised at Morehouse Farm in New York State. Merino wool is highly valued for its fineness and softness. The scarf Nick's wearing at left was made with three 2-ounce (approximately 145-yard) skeins of yarn and is 88 inches long, which means it can be wrapped around your neck a few times. The same style of scarf can be made with 2 skeins of yarn, and it will still be plenty long.

materials

- 290 to 435 yards bulky yarn, such as 3-Strand Morehouse Merino
- 1 pair size 10 knitting needles (or whatever size feels comfortable—the smaller the needles, the more the ribbing will pull in)
- Yarn needle

directions

Cast on 39 stitches.

Row 1: Knit 3, purl 3. Repeat to end of row, ending with knit 3.

Row 2: Purl 3, knit 3. Repeat to end of row, ending with purl 3.

Repeat rows 1 and 2 until the scarf is the length you want it to be. Cast off in pattern (this means that you should continue to knit the knit stitches and purl the purl stitches when you are transferring the stitches from the left to the right needle in the cast-off row). Using the yarn needle, weave in any loose ends.

knitting in the round

Knitting tubular shapes in the round can be done on circular or double-pointed needles. A lot of people prefer knitting in the round (also called circular knitting) to knitting flat because it requires less finishing work. When you knit in the round, you don't usually have to sew pieces of knitted fabric together. Also, when you work stockinette stitch in the round, you don't need to purl, because the front (knit) side of the work is always facing you. In instructions for circular knitting, the word "row" is replaced by the word "round," because instead of knitting flat, you're now knitting in circles.

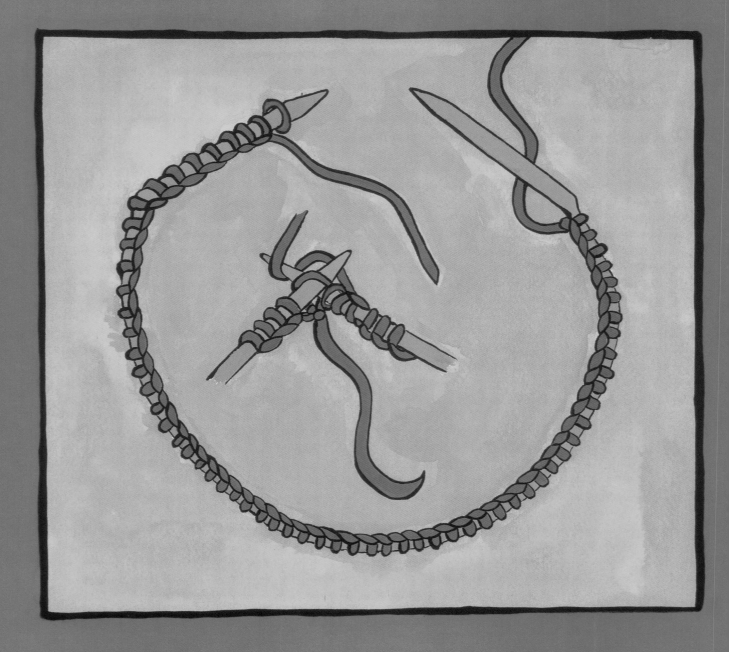

knitting in the round
on circular needles

Circular needles look like 2 short straight needles with a flexible cord in the middle. They can be used in the same way as straight needles to knit flat fabrics or they can be used to knit tubular shapes, such as the body of the backpack shown on page 84. Circular needles come in different lengths. When you are knitting in the round with them, you need to choose the correct length so that the first and last stitches you cast on can be joined to each other to make a circle. If your needles are too long, the circle won't close. If your needles are too short, you won't have enough room for all of your stitches.

If your needles are the correct length but you're still having trouble joining the stitches to knit the first round, simply knit the first few rows flat (just as you would on straight needles), then join the first and last stitches to make a circle once you have 1 or 2 inches of knitted fabric finished. At this point it will be easier to see what you are doing. Remember to sew together the open seam later on.

1 Cast on in the same way you cast on for straight needles. Slide the stitches so that they are spread out evenly from the point of the first needle around the flexible cord to the point of the other needle. Place a stitch marker on top of the first cast-on stitch. Lay the needles on a flat surface so that they make a circle with the first and last stitches meeting at the top of the circle (with the last cast-on stitch and the working yarn on the right and the first cast-on stitch and the marker on the left). Make sure that the cast-on edge is in the inside of the circle. It is very important that the cast-on edge is not twisted!

2 Pick up the needles, slip the marker from the left needle to the right needle, and begin knitting the first stitch that you casted on (on the left needle), pulling tightly on the working yarn (which is coming from the right needle) so that you do not end up with a large gap where the stitches from the right needle meet the stitches from the left needle. Knit all the way around. When you reach the marker, slip it to the right needle and continue. Each time you slip the marker you will know that you are about to start a new round.

knitting in the round
on 4 double-pointed needles

Knitting in the round on 4 double-pointed needles is not difficult but it takes a little time to get used to. The hardest part is holding all of the needles for the first few rounds. After these rounds are done, the knitted fabric keeps the needles in place and you only need to pay attention to 2 needles at a time, just as if you were knitting flat. If you can, ask an experienced knitter to help you in the beginning. Or work the first few rows on straight needles and divide the stitches onto 3 needles once you have 1 or 2 inches of knitted fabric that you can hold. It should be easier to join the stitches at this point. When you are done with the rest of the project, sew together the open seam.

1 Cast on the number of stitches called for in the pattern on 1 double-pointed needle. Make sure your stitches are secure—not too loose and not too tight. They should not slip off the needle if you hold the needle at 1 end but they should not be so tight that you cannot move them when you want to move them.

2 Divide the stitches evenly among the 3 needles (the one on which you casted on and 2 others) and lay them on a flat surface so that they make a triangle shape. Arrange the needles so that the first and last stitches you casted on meet at the top of the triangle. The first stitches you casted on should be on the needle on the left and the last stitches you casted on and the working yarn should be on the needle on the right. Make sure the cast-on edge is in the inside of the triangle.

3 Lift up the 3 needles with both hands, keeping them in the triangle shape. Shift the needles so that they are all in your left hand, then with the fourth (empty) needle and your right hand, begin knitting the first stitch that you casted on, pulling the working yarn tightly so that you do not end up with a large gap where the stitches from 1 needle meet the stitches from the next needle. Continue knitting to the end of the first needle.

4 Using the empty needle, knit the stitches from the second needle. Using the empty needle, knit the stitches from the third needle, placing a marker between the last and the second-to-last stitch. You are now back where you started. Continue knitting in the round until the tube you are creating is the length you want it to be.

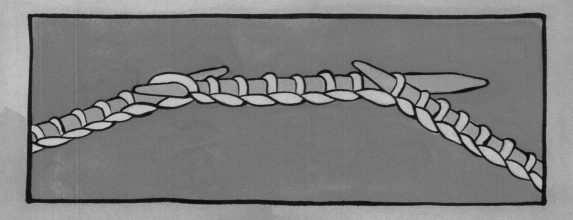

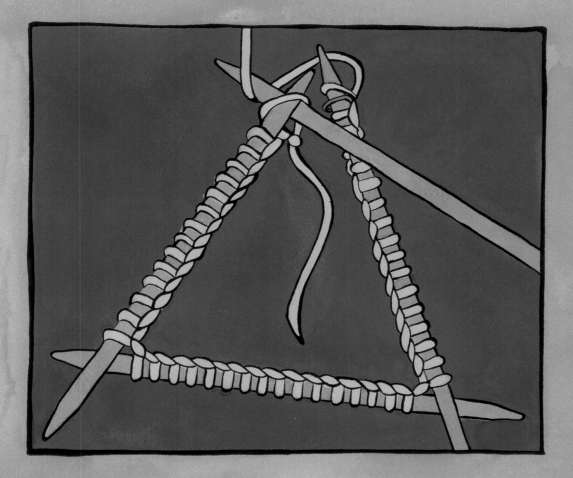

backpacks & more

Imagine carrying your lunch to school in a backpack like the ones worn by Manon and Emily, a backpack you knitted yourself. You might even start a trend among your friends. The purse/wallet and eyeglass/pen case on page 89 are great accessories to the backpack, but they're also useful by themselves. They're quick to knit and make great little gifts.

The yarn used to make the blue backpack worn by Manon in the photo at left is recycled. Before wool is machine-spun to make yarn, it is combed in a carding machine so that all the fibers line up in the same direction. Some of the fibers remain in the machine or fall to the floor. This leftover, uncombed fiber used to be thrown away, but now it's collected to make recycled yarns.

materials

· · · · · · · · ·

Approximately 220 yards bulky yarn, such as Rowan Recycled Chunky or Chunky Tweed

Approximately 110 yards bulky yarn, such as Rowan Recycled Chunky or Chunky Tweed, in a contrasting color

1 size 9 24-inch circular needle (or whatever size 24-inch circular needle feels comfortable)

3 buttons, each approximately 1 inch in diameter

1 wooden bead or ring with a hole large enough for both cords to fit through snugly (hole should be approximately ⅝ inch), for backpack (available at arts and crafts stores; if you cannot find a bead you like, make one with polymer clay)

Stitch marker

Yarn needle

Knitting spool or 2 double-pointed needles to make the cord for the backpack and purse

Sewing needle and thread

Scrap yarn or safety pin

directions

to make the backpack

for the bottom of the pack

With your main color of yarn and circular needle, cast on 34 stitches. Work back and forth in garter stitch (knit every row) until the piece measures 4½ inches. Bind off.

for the body of the pack

1 The body of the backpack is knit in the round. With the main color of yarn and circular needle, cast on 102 stitches. Join the first and last stitch and knit the first round, being careful not to twist the stitches when you join them. Place a marker between the first and last stitches to mark the beginning of the round. Work until the piece measures 5 inches long.

2 Take your gauge by measuring with a ruler the number of stitches in a 4-inch-wide section of the pack. The gauge of the backpacks in the photograph is 14 stitches over 4 inches (or 3½ stitches per inch). The exact size of this backpack is not important, so you do not have to match the gauge exactly, but you should try to be close to make sure you don't run out of yarn. If you are knitting very loosely (fewer than 3 stitches per inch) you may not have enough yarn for the backpack and the accessories.

3 Continue to knit in the round until the body of the pack measures 10 inches long.

for the drawstring holes

1 Bind off 2 stitches at the beginning of the next round (if you have forgotten how to bind off, see page 33), then knit 3 stitches. Repeat (bind off 2, knit 3) all the way around.

2 Knit the next round, casting on 2 stitches over the bound-off stitches of the previous round. You should have 17 holes for the drawstring.

3 Knit 1 round. Bind off the first 68 stitches of the next round (you should have 34 stitches remaining on your needles).

for the flap

1 To make the flap, work flat (back and forth, not in the round). With the second color of yarn, work in garter stitch (knit every row) until the flap measures 4½ inches.

2 To make the buttonhole in the flap, knit 16 stitches, bind off 2 stitches (as for the drawstring), then knit the remaining 15 stitches.

3 Knit 16 stitches, then cast on 2 stitches over the bound-off stitches from the previous row. Continue in garter stitch (knit every row) until the flap measures 6 inches. Bind off all stitches.

making i-cord

The straps on both the backpack and the purse are made with knitted cord
that can be created with either a knitting spool or 2 double-pointed needles. This kind of
cord was nicknamed i-cord by Elizabeth Zimmermann, a very famous knitter
with a good sense of humor. The "i" actually stands for "idiot," a reference to how
easy this cord is to make. Directions for making i-cord with a knitting spool
are on page 19. The instructions below are for making i-cord with 2 double-pointed needles.
The thicker the yarn and the more stitches you cast on, the thicker the i-cord.

1 Cast on a few stitches. (For the back-pack and purse cord, cast on 3 or 4 stitches.) Knit to the end of the row.

2 Slide the stitches to the "bottom" tip of the needle. Turn the needle so that the "bottom" becomes the "top." The working yarn should now be coming from the bottom stitch.

3 Knit the stitches again, pulling the working yarn up from the bottom stitch when you knit the first stitch (this is shown in the illustration).

4 Repeat steps 2 and 3 until the cord is the length you want it to be. It takes a couple of rows before you are able to see the cord forming. Before that, it may look as though you are creating a big knot instead of a cord.

for the drawstring/i-cord

With the second color of yarn and a knitting spool or 2 double-pointed needles, make a 55-inch i-cord drawstring. If using double-pointed needles, cast on 3 or 4 stitches. See page 87 for instructions on making i-cord.

finishing

1 Thread the yarn needle with the main color of yarn and sew the bottom of the pack to the body, beginning at 1 corner so that the back of the pack (the side with the flap along the top edge) is sewn to a long edge of the bottom.

2 Find the drawstring hole centered under the flap. Pull the cord from the outside of the backpack in through the hole, then out through the next hole (in either direction). Work in and out of the holes all the way around, exiting a second time from the center hole (the hole where you started). Pull both ends of the cord together through the ring or bead.

3 Attach the end of the left cord to the lower left corner of the pack by securely sewing 1½ inches of the cord to the pack. Repeat with the right end of the cord on the right side.

4 Find the spot on the pack where the buttonhole falls when you fold over the flap. Mark it with a piece of yarn or a safety pin. Sew a button to the marked spot on the pack. Weave in all loose ends.

to make the eyeglass/pen case

1 Even though the eyeglass/pen case is knit flat (back and forth, not in the round), you can make it with the circular needle used to make the backpack. With the main color of yarn, cast on 32 stitches. Work in garter stitch (knit every row) until the piece measures 1½ inches.

2 Make a buttonhole as follows: Knit 3, then bind off 2 stitches. Knit the remaining stitches in the row. Work in garter stitch in the next row, casting on 2 stitches over the 2 stitches bound off in the previous row.

3 Continue working in garter stitch until the piece measures 3 inches, stopping at the end of the case with the buttonhole. In the next row, bind off 8 stitches, then work the remaining 24 stitches in garter stitch for 3 inches. Bind off all stitches.

4 Fold the case in half lengthwise and sew the side seam using the overcast stitch or mattress stitch (see page 37). Weave in any loose ends of yarn. Find the spot on the case that matches the buttonhole on the flap. Mark it with a piece of yarn or a safety pin, then sew a button to the marked spot.

to make the purse/wallet

for the body

Even though the purse/wallet is knit flat, it can also be made with circular needles. Using the main color of yarn, cast on 20 stitches. Work in garter stitch (knit every row) for 9 inches.

for the flap

1. Change to the second color of yarn and work in garter stitch for 1½ inches.

2. On the next row, make a buttonhole as follows: Knit 9, bind off the next 2 stitches, knit 8. Knit the next row, casting on 2 stitches over the 2 stitches bound off in the previous row. Continue to work in garter stitch until the flap measures 3 inches total. Bind off.

for the strap/i-cord

If you are making the wallet, skip this step. With the second color of yarn and a knitting spool or 2 double-pointed needles, make an i-cord strap that is about 45 inches long or the length you want it to be. Directions for making i-cord are on page 87.

finishing

Fold the body of the purse or wallet in half, not including the flap. Sew together the sides using the overcast or mattress stitch. Weave in any loose ends of yarn. Sew on the button. If you are making the purse, match 1 end of the cord with the bottom edge of the purse and sew the cord to the purse along the side seam. Repeat on the other side of the purse.

Wizard's cap

The Wizard's Cap is started on circular needles and finished on double-pointed needles. If you can, use double-pointed needles made out of wood instead of metal or plastic—the yarn will slip around less. If you are making a striped cap, always start the new color at the beginning of a round.

Up to this point, you have taken your gauge (measured the number of stitches per inch) for practice purposes only. Because the previous projects did-n't need to be a specific size, you didn't need to worry about knitting at a specific gauge. But you'll want the Wizard's Cap to fit snugly on your head, so for this project you'll need to match the gauge—5 stitches per inch—pretty closely, if not exactly. Following the directions, knit up to the crown, then check your gauge.

materials

. . . .

Approximately 190 yards worsted-weight yarn, such as Classic Elite Tapestry

1 size 6 16-inch circular needle

4 or 5 size 6 double-pointed needles, preferably wooden

6 stitch markers (1 of the 6 should be a different color from the others)

Yarn needle

Adult-Sized Wizard's Cap

. . . .

To make this cap for an adult, cast on 108 stitches instead of 102. When it is time to decrease for the crown, instead of starting with knit 15, knit 2 together, start with knit 16, knit 2 together.

directions

taking your gauge

The gauge for the Wizard's Cap is 5 stitches to 1 inch (or 20 stitches to 4 inches). The best way to take your gauge for this project is simply to start knitting your hat. After you have completed the body of the cap, before decreasing for the crown, place the work on a flat surface and measure the number of stitches you have knit over 4 inches. If your gauge is a little bit off (between 19½ and 20½ stitches over 4 inches), the cap will probably still fit because it is stretchy. But if you have far fewer or far more stitches per inch you are going to have to decide whether to finish it and risk having it not fit you (you can always give the hat away to someone with a bigger or smaller head!) or to rip out what you have done and start over with different-sized needles. Try larger needles if your hat is too small and smaller needles if it's too big.

If you want to take your gauge more quickly, you can knit a flat swatch (cast on 25 stitches using size 6 needles, work back and forth in stockinette stitch for about 4½ inches, then count the number of stitches you are knitting over 4 inches), but the truth is that your gauge will probably be a little bit different when you knit the cap. That is because the cap is knit in the round and when you knit in the round your gauge is usually different than when you knit flat.

to make the body of the hat

Using circular needles, cast on 102 stitches. Working back and forth (as you would on straight needles), knit 1 row, purl 1 row, knit 2 rows. Join the first and last stitches so that you are knitting in the round. Be sure not to twist the work—the knitted fabric should be on the inside of the circle. Knit 1 round, then place the different-colored marker between the first and last stitches of the round. Knit 18 more rounds. If you are making a striped cap, change colors at the beginning of a round. Purl 3 rounds (this will make a narrow ridge like the one at the bottom of the cap). Knit 1 round. At this point, you will have worked 23 rounds. Do not count the bottom ridge, which you knit flat, when counting the rounds.

to decrease for the crown

Round 24: *Knit 15 stitches, decrease by knitting the next 2 stitches together, then place a marker on the right needle.* Repeat the instruction between the asterisks 5 more times, which will bring you to the end of the round (where the odd-colored marker is located). You will now have 96 stitches on your needles. Keep all the markers on the needles.

Round 25: Knit all the way around, slipping the markers as you come to them.

Round 26: *Knit 14 stitches, then decrease by knitting 2 stitches together, then slip the marker to the right needle.* Repeat the instruction between the asterisks 5 more times, which will bring you to the end of the round. You will now have 90 stitches on your needles.

Round 27: Knit all the way around.

Round 28: *Knit 13 stitches, then decrease by knitting 2 stitches together.* Repeat the instruction between the asterisks 5 more times, which will bring you to the end of the round. You will now have 84 stitches on your needles.

Continue to work, decreasing every other round, knitting 1 stitch less before knitting 2 together until 12 stitches remain. When the stitches will no longer reach around the circular needle, switch to double-pointed needles. To do this, simply knit off the circular needle onto 1 double-pointed needle at a time, dividing the stitches evenly among 3 or 4 needles. Remember that you need to leave 1 needle (a 4th or 5th needle) empty.

to make the i-cord stem

Round 1: At this point, you will have 12 stitches divided evenly on 3 or 4 double-pointed needles. To continue, decrease by knitting 2 stitches together 6 times, which will bring you to the end of the round. You will have 6 stitches on your needles when you finish the round.

Round 2: Knit 1 round.

Row 3 and all remaining rows: Put all the stitches on 1 double-pointed needle, making sure that the working yarn is at the tip of the needle (not in the middle). With a second double-pointed needle, knit 1, knit 2 stitches together, knit 1, knit 2 stitches together. You will have 4 stitches on your needle when you finish the row. One side of the stitches is flat, and the other side is bumpy.

With the flat side of the stitches facing you, knit 4. Don't turn the work to the wrong (bumpy) side. Work the i-cord on the double-pointed needles until it measures 4 inches (see page 87 for instructions on making i-cord).

Cut the yarn, leaving a tail of about 4 inches. With the yarn needle, draw the tail through the 4 stitches. Insert the tip of the yarn needle (with the tail of yarn) a few inches down into the center of the i-cord so that most of the yarn is hidden inside it, then pull the yarn needle out the side. Remove the needle and snip off any leftover tail. Tie the i-cord in a knot close to the crown of the hat. Stitch together the seam at the bottom of the hat.

magic spiral tube socks

Like magic, these sassy spiral socks fit comfortably on most feet even though there is no special sizing or shaping. They're knit in the round on 4 needles. They start with a rib of knit 3, purl 3, which creates an elastic "band" at the top of the socks to hold them up on the legs. The rib is then shifted so that it moves 1 stitch to the right every round. The result? A diagonal spiral that twists and travels down the socks.

To make the Magic Spiral Tube Socks in an adult or child size you will need approximately 285 yards of worsted-weight yarn. If you want to make striped socks, buy whatever colors you like, or use leftovers from other projects. Just remember that all the yarn needs to be a similar weight and thickness. To decide on the order of the different-colored stripes before knitting, wrap approximately 12-inch strands of yarn several times around the short side of a long, narrow piece of cardboard. Change the order of the colors on the cardboard until you come up with a combination you like. If possible, use double-pointed needles made out of wood instead of metal or plastic. The yarn will slip around less on wooden needles.

materials

· · · · · · · · · · · ·

Approximately 285 yards worsted-weight yarn, such as Classic Elite Tapestry (this is enough for 1 pair of child- or adult-sized socks)

4 size 6 double-pointed needles

Stitch marker

Yarn needle

directions

taking your gauge

The best way to take your gauge for this project is simply to start knitting the first sock. After you have completed about 4½ inches of the diagonal ribbing, place the work on a flat surface and measure the number of stitches you have knit over 4 inches. Do not include the edge stitches in your measurement and do not round off fractions. For these socks you want to be knitting 18 stitches over 4 inches (or 4½ stitches per inch). If your gauge is a little bit off (between 17 and 19 stitches over 4 inches), the socks will probably still fit because of the elasticity of ribbing.

for the body of the socks

1 Cast on 42 stitches on 1 of the double-pointed needles. Divide the 42 stitches onto 3 needles (14 stitches per needle) and place a marker between the last and second-to-last stitch on the third needle.

2 Start the first round by knitting the first cast-on stitch with the fourth needle, pulling tightly on the yarn coming from the third needle so that you do not end up with a large gap where the stitches from 1 needle meet the stitches from the next needle. See page 83 for a clear illustration of this process. Work in a knit 3, purl 3 rib for about 12 rounds.

Or, if you are having trouble joining the stitches so that you can knit in the round, cast on 42 stitches and work back and forth in the knit 3, purl 3 rib for about 12 rounds, then divide the stitches onto the 3 double-pointed needles. It should be easier to join the stitches now that you have a few inches of knitted fabric to hold.

3 Begin the spiral pattern by knitting the first 2 stitches. Next, increase 1 stitch by knitting into the third stitch twice (see page 50 if you need an explanation of this technique). Purl 2. From this point on, work in a knit 3, purl 3 rib until the sock measures approximately 12½ inches. If you are making striped socks, change colors at the beginning of the round. In the last round, decrease by knitting 2 stitches together once at any point. You will now have 42 stitches divided among 3 needles.

for the toe

4 **Round 1:** Knit 4, decrease 1 by knitting 2 stitches together. Repeat all the way around. (When you finish the round, you will have 35 stitches divided on the 3 needles.)

Round 2: Knit all the way around.

Round 3: Knit 3, decrease 1 by knitting 2 stitches together. Repeat all the way around. (When you finish the round, you will have 28 stitches divided on the 3 needles.)

Round 4: Knit all the way around.

Round 5: Knit 2, decrease 1 by knitting 2 stitches together. Repeat all the way around. (When you finish the round, you will have 21 stitches divided on the 3 needles.)

Round 6: Knit all the way around.

Round 7: Knit 1, decrease 1 by knitting 2 stitches together. Repeat all the way around. (When you finish the round, you will have 14 stitches divided on the 3 needles.)

Round 8: Knit all the way around.

Round 9: Decrease by knitting 2 stitches together all the way around. (When you finish the round, you will have 7 stitches divided on 3 needles.)

5 Cut the yarn, leaving a 6-inch tail. Thread the tail onto the yarn needle and draw it through the remaining 7 stitches to close the sock. Bring the tail to the inside of the sock and weave in the end. If you started your sock by knitting back and forth, sew up the open seam at the top. Then repeat all directions to make a second sock.

knitting around the world

People have been knitting for centuries all over the world, especially in places that are cold in the winter, because people have always needed a way to stay warm. Some countries are well known for specific styles of knitting. When we learn about different types of knitting, we are able to become armchair travelers: We can visit any country in the world in our minds, without ever leaving the comfort of our own homes.

ireland is known for a kind of textured sweater called the Aran. It is named after the Aran Islands, where this kind of sweater was first made. Aran sweaters have lots of cables. A cable is a knitting term for stitches that are combined to look like ropes twisted together. Greece and Portugal are also known for similar sweaters.

A Scottish island called **fair isle**, which is part of the Shetland Islands, is well known for a special style of multicolored knitting. The colors are combined to create lots of different shapes, such as OXOs (pronounced "ox-ohs," and looking like the letters). Fair Isle patterns are traditionally worked into sweaters as well as vests, gloves, and hats. Knitters in the Shetland Islands like to knit with wool yarn from the sheep, also called Shetlands, that live on their land.

People on Fair Isle and the other **shetland islands** also like to make beautiful lace shawls into which they knit the shapes of the nature around them, such as sea shells and ocean waves. This kind of lace is known as Shetland lace.

Lace is also very popular in **russia**, where people knit snowflake and ice-crystal shapes into their shawls, which are often made from mohair and cashmere, fibers that grow on the goats that live there.

In **scandinavia** (a region of the world that includes Denmark, Norway, Sweden, Finland, and Iceland), knitters often make sweaters with images of reindeer and snowflakes on them.

latvia, a tiny country located between Estonia in the north and Lithuania in the south, is known for its multicolored mittens. The shapes knitted into the mittens are often related to ancient mythology and have names like moon, morning star, sun, and firecross. Sometimes these mittens flare out at the bottom (wrist) edge and sometimes the edges are fringed.

In **south america**, a lot of knitters make ch'ullus—bright multicolored hats with small shapes knit into them and triangular earflaps. People there also knit small dolls and purses and fancy arm warmers called maquitos, which they wear on special occasions.

In the **middle east**, in places like Greece, Turkey, and Egypt, people have been known to knit beautiful multicolored socks. Often, they start knitting their socks at the toe, then knit the entire sock except for the heel, which they insert at the very end. In the United States, it is more common for knitters to start their socks at the top of the leg,

then work down to the heel and around to the toe.

In coastal areas of **washington state** and **british columbia**, Native Americans are known for their sweaters made with undyed wool. They are called Salish sweaters, after the tribe that first knit them, and usually feature a series of horizontal stripes. Into each stripe a knitter works different shapes, such as animals, leaves, flowers, or geometric forms, including the OXOs that are used in Fair Isle knitting.

new stitch patterns

If you love playing with colors and textures, you'll never get bored with knitting, because you'll never run out of ways to combine different colors of yarn and knit and purl stitches. You already know garter, stockinette, and reverse stockinette stitch, and ribbing: Other knit and purl variations, such as seed, basketweave, simple cable, and checkerboard stitch, offer brand new knitting possibilities. To practice these stitch patterns, you can knit sample swatches and add them along with your sketches and comments to a notebook, or make more bean bags, or combine all the patterns in a funky Swatch Scarf.

swatch scarf

You can create this colorful scarf just by practicing different stitch patterns. It's actually 1 long swatch of switching stitches, including 9 new patterns featured on the next few pages. Swatches are sample pieces of fabric that are usually used as tests for larger projects, but, in this case, the swatches *are* the project. Make your scarf unique by picking your own colors and trying the stitch patterns in your own order, repeating those you like best or need to practice. Then wrap it around your neck while it is still on the needles to decide how long you want it to be.

directions

materials

- - - - - - - - - - - -

A few different colors of worsted-weight or bulky yarn, such as Classic Elite Montera

1 pair size 8 knitting needles (or whatever size feels comfortable)

Yarn needle

Cast on 40 stitches. Choose a stitch pattern from pages 105–107 and work for at least 4 inches. When ready, choose another stitch pattern and/or color. Repeat until the scarf is the length you want it to be. Bind off. Fold the scarf in half lengthwise with the right side facing out and stitch together the 3 open sides using the mattress stitch (page 37). Or, fold the scarf in half lengthwise with the wrong side facing out and stitch together 1 short side and the long side using the overcast stitch (page 37). Turn the scarf right side out, then stitch together the open short end. Your scarf will look neater if it is stitched together using the mattress stitch.

Keeping a Swatch Notebook

By now, you've had a lot of chances to make swatches. You may have made square swatches and sewn them together into bean bags or you may have knit 1 long, ever-changing swatch that you transformed into a scarf. Another idea is to put together a swatch notebook. Choose a sturdy notebook with pages large enough for your swatches, and attach a different swatch to each page with staples or by sewing down the corners. On the same page or the facing page, record the name of the stitch and how it is formed. For example, for the stockinette stitch you would write something like "Knit 1 row, purl 1 row, repeat." To make your swatch notebook even more useful, also include the name of the yarn, the needle size you used, and the gauge. Consider making swatches of the same stitch pattern in different types of yarn, in different color combinations, and with different size needles. It will be interesting for you to see how the look of the finished swatches changes. Use your swatch notebook for knitting experiments and as a reference tool when you are creating new projects.

playing with stitch patterns

Use these stitch patterns to make bean bags, a swatch scarf, or pieces for your swatch notebook. If you are making a bean bag or an individual swatch, cast on 20 stitches, knit in the stitch pattern of your choice until you have a square, then bind off. If you are making a swatch scarf, cast on 40 stitches, knit for 4 inches or more, then switch to a new stitch pattern and continue knitting.

striped garter stitch

Work in garter stitch (knit every row). When ready to start or finish a stripe, change colors at the beginning of a row.

striped stockinette

Work in stockinette stitch (knit 1 row, purl 1 row, repeat). When ready to start or finish a stripe, change colors at the beginning of a row.

reverse stockinette

Work in stockinette stitch (knit 1 row, purl 1 row, repeat), but treat the bumpy, purl side as the front. If making a scarf, start your first knit row on the wrong side of the scarf.

checkerboard

When working with 2 colors in 1 row, it is easy for the yarns to get tangled. To avoid this problem, work with small balls of yarn. When ready to switch from 1 color to another, simply drop the first color and pick up the second, making sure that you always carry the working yarns in back on the knit rows and in front on the purl rows.

Row 1: Knit 2 in color A, knit 2 in color B, repeat these 4 stitches across the row.

Row 2: Purl 2 in color B, purl 2 in color A, repeat these 4 stitches across the row.

Row 3: Knit 2 in color B, knit 2 in color A, repeat these 4 stitches across the row.

Row 4: Purl 2 in color A, purl 2 in color B, repeat these 4 stitches across the row.

Repeat these 4 rows until you are ready to bind off or choose another stitch pattern.

seed stitch

Row 1: Knit 1, purl 1, repeat across the row.

Row 2: Purl 1, knit 1, repeat across the row.

Repeat these 2 rows until ready to bind off or choose another stitch pattern. Note that you are always knitting on top of purl stitches and purling on top of knit stitches.

striped garter stitch

striped stockinette

reverse stockinette

checkerboard

stockinette with
reverse stockinette ridges

seed stitch

basketweave

2-by-2 ribbing

simple cable

stockinette with reverse stockinette ridges

This is a variation of the stitch pattern used to make the Crazy Caterpillar on page 73.

Rows 1–4: Work in stockinette stitch (knit 1 row, purl 1 row, repeat) in color A for 4 rows.

Rows 5–6: Knit in color B for 2 rows.

Row 7: Purl in color B.

Row 8: Knit in color B.

Rows 9–12: Switch to color A and work in stockinette stitch for 4 rows, starting with a knit row.

Rows 13–14: Knit in color C for 2 rows.

Row 15: Purl in color C.

Row 16: Knit in color C.

Rows 17–20: Switch to color A and work in stockinette stitch for 4 rows, starting with a knit row.

Rows 21 and 22: Knit in color D for 2 rows.

Row 23: Purl in color D.

Row 24: Knit in color D.

Rows 25–28: Switch to color A and work in stockinette stitch for 4 rows, starting with a knit row.

Repeat these 28 rows until ready to bind off or choose another stitch pattern.

simple cable

To make a simple cable, you will need a cable needle or a double-pointed needle in addition to your regular knitting needles. In row 3, when instructed, you will slip 3 stitches, 1 at a time, onto the cable needle (or double-pointed needle), inserting the needle into the top of the stitches as if you are going to purl them, but instead of purling them you are simply going to transfer them from the left needle to the cable needle. Then, when instructed, you will knit them off the cable needle. Follow the numbers in the parentheses if you are making the swatch scarf. If only 1 number is given, it applies to both the scarf and the bean bag.

Row 1: Purl 7 (17), knit 6, purl 7 (17).

Row 2: Knit 7 (17), purl 6, knit 7 (17).

Row 3: Purl 7 (17), slip the next 3 stitches onto the cable needle, and let the needle hang in the front of the work. Knit the next 3 stitches off the left needle, then knit the 3 stitches off the cable needle (knitting the stitches off the cable needle in the same order that you slipped them on). Purl the remaining 7 (17) stitches on the left needle.

Row 4: Knit 7 (17), purl 6, knit 7 (17). Repeat these 4 rows until ready to bind off or choose another stitch pattern.

basketweave

Rows 1–5: Knit 5, purl 5, repeat across the row.

Rows 6–10: Purl 5, knit 5, repeat across the row. Repeat these 10 rows until ready to choose another stitch pattern or bind off, ending after you have completed either a row 5 or a row 10.

2-by-2 ribbing

All rows: Knit 2, purl 2, repeat across the row.

fuzzy felt balls

When you wash wool, you work gently and with a consistent water temperature. To felt wool, you do the opposite, shocking the fibers by changing the temperature of the water often and agitating the fibers by rubbing them back and forth constantly. Almost anything made of 100% wool can be felted. Sometimes, knitters make articles such as mittens, hats, or bags in an extra-large size, then felt them to make them smaller, stronger, and impermeable (which means liquid can't pass through them). During felting, the tiny fibers that make up wool interlock, tightening and closing the small holes that are a natural part of the knitted fabric. Felt can be beautiful when you make it on purpose, but it can be upsetting when you make it by mistake, such as when you accidentally put a wool sweater in a washing machine and it shrinks so much you can't wear it anymore.

Making felt balls is a great way to begin to understand the felting process. You start with wool that has been carded (meaning it has been combed so that all of the fibers lie in the same direction) but not spun into yarn or knit, plus some dishwashing liquid and a couple of bowls.

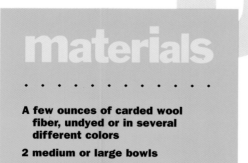

materials

- **A few ounces of carded wool fiber, undyed or in several different colors**
- **2 medium or large bowls**
- **Liquid soap, such as soap for handwashing dishes**

directions

1 To prepare the wool for felting you will need to pull the fibers apart a little bit. Otherwise you'll end up with clumps of felted wool that do not stick together in a ball. Take a small handful of wool and gently pull on the fibers so that they loosen and you can see a lot of light through them. Roll the loosened fibers into a small, very tight ball, changing the direction in which you roll often (the action is really a combination of rolling and folding). Continue to add loosened fiber (in the same color or different colors) and roll, handful by handful, until you have a ball that is a little bit larger than the size you want to end up with (your ball will shrink slightly when you felt it). Set the ball aside. If the ball wants to unroll, place something heavy on top of it.

2 Place both bowls in a large sink or bathtub. Fill 1 bowl with cold water and some ice. Fill the other bowl with very hot tap water (as hot as you can stand touching with your hands). Add enough soap to 1 of the bowls to make a lot of suds.

3 Dunk your ball into the bowl with the sudsy water. Begin rolling the wet ball around in your hands as if you are making a meatball. After about a minute, dunk the ball into the other bowl and, again, roll it around in your hands like a meatball. Squirt a little more soap directly onto the ball. Continue dunking and rolling the ball for approximately 5 to 15 minutes, until it hardens and all the fibers on the surface are sticking to it. You can agitate the wool fibers even more (and shorten the felting time) by running hot and cold water from the faucet over the ball. The trick is to continually switch back and forth between very hot and very cold water. This is not an exact science. Experiment to find the method that works best for you by varying how often you switch from hot to cold, how much soap you use, and how roughly you handle the ball.

4 When the ball is completely felted, squeeze it hard to get rid of extra water. The ball will still be soapy. Set aside to dry.

Playing with Color

Experimenting with different combinations of colors is fun and interesting. Many knitters spend a lot of time at yarn shops and at home arranging yarns next to each other to see which colors they like best together. You can try that or you can play a similar game with a large box of crayons. To start, pick 5 different crayons and draw a thick line with each one, keeping the lines close to each other. Next pick 5 more colors and draw lines again nearby on the same piece of paper. Continue to do this with different colors a few more times. Now take a few moments to study your artwork. Which color combinations do you like best? Do certain combinations remind you of anything in particular, such as fall or spring, the ocean, or a field of flowers? Do certain combinations make you feel happy or sad? Color is amazing. It can even affect your mood.

Now draw a new group of colors, then draw the same group again but without 1 of the colors. Did taking that single color away have any effect on the whole group? Next, take away a second color, or replace 1 of the colors with another color. For more surprises, try picking colors with your eyes closed.

Five is a good number of colors to start with but it is not a magic number in this game. Combine as many colors as you like, from 2 to 10 or more. If you play this game with friends, you'll find that everyone responds to colors in different ways. It's not unusual for 1 person to love a color combination and another person not to like that combination at all. When it comes to color, there are no rules or limits. Combine colors in any way you like.

your first sweater

The time has come to knit your first sweater. While the Curly-Edge Pullover is not hard to make, it will take longer to finish than the other projects, so work on it when you have big chunks of time, on weekends, rainy days spent indoors, or during long car trips. To make sure the sweater will fit the way you like, you need to determine the correct size and then make a gauge swatch. Instructions for these 2 tasks appear at the start of the pattern. But in books written for more experienced knitters, this information is not given. Instead it's assumed that you will complete these steps before you begin any project.

curly-edge pullover

This sweater takes advantage of the fact that stockinette stitch curls naturally. In the process of making the Curly-Edge Pullover, you will learn several new techniques, including a new way to decrease, how to pick up stitches around a neckline in order to add a collar, and how to give a handknit sweater a finished, professional look. Sasha, Emily, and Manon at left, along with Stanley and Nick on page 112, are all sporting variations of this comfortable, oversized, roll-neck sweater: Sasha put on a red Curly-Edge Cap to complete her fashionable ensemble. (Instructions for the cap, written in standard abbreviations, are on page 121.)

materials

. . . .

- **Approximately 875, (1000, 1125, 1250) yards bulky yarn for a solid-color sweater (buy about 125 yards extra if making a sweater with stripes in 3 or more colors), such as Brown Sheep Company's Lamb's Pride Bulky or Morehouse Farm Wind Dancer Merino**
- **1 pair each size 8 and 10½ knitting needles, or size needed to obtain gauge**
- **1 size 8 16-inch circular needle, or size needed to obtain gauge**
- **2 stitch holders**
- **Yarn needle**

size

Children's sizes 8 (10, 12, 14)

finished measurements

Chest at underarm: 37 (40, 43, 46) inches
Length from shoulder: 21 (23, 25, 26) inches
Sleeve length: 14 (15, 16, 17) inches

gauge

14 stitches to 4 inches using larger needles over stockinette stitch

directions

to determine your size

The easiest way to determine your size is to use a favorite sweatshirt or sweater as a guide. Lay the chosen garment on a flat surface and measure across from underarm to underarm. This will give you half the chest measurement. Now multiply that measurement by 2 and refer to the measurements at the beginning of the pattern. For example, if your sweatshirt measured 20 inches across, its chest measurement would be 40 inches. To make the Curly-Edge Pullover you would follow the instructions for a size 10 sweater. If the measurement you get from your sweatshirt falls between 2 sizes, round it off to the next larger size. Remember that the Curly-Edge Pullover is an oversized sweater—it's supposed to be very roomy.

This pattern is written for a solid-color sweater in 4 sizes. So you don't get confused, using a pencil, circle all of the numbers that refer to your size before you start. For example, if you are making this sweater in a size 8, you will circle the first number (the number outside of the parentheses). If you are making this sweater in a size 12, you will circle the third number (which is the second number inside the parentheses). Do this very carefully, then double-check your work.

to make a gauge swatch

Using size 10½ needles, cast on 18 stitches and work in stockinette stitch until you have a piece of knitting that measures at least 4½ inches. Bind off. Pin your swatch to a flat surface, such as to a towel spread out on a table, and measure the number of stitches you have knit over 4 inches. (Do not include the edge stitches in your measurement and do not round off fractions.) For this sweater you want to be knitting 14 stitches to 4 inches (or 3½ stitches per inch). If you have more than 14 stitches over 4 inches, make another swatch with needles that are 1 or 2 sizes larger. If you have fewer than 14 stitches over 4 inches, make another swatch with needles that are 1 or 2 sizes smaller. Continue making swatches until you reach the correct gauge. (If you like, use your swatches to make bean bags [see page 35] or put them in a swatch notebook [see page 104].) Once you have decided on a main needle size, subtract 2 to determine the smaller needle size used for the first 2 inches of the front, back, and sleeves and for the collar.

to make the pullover

to make the back

With the smaller needles, cast on 65 (71, 75, 81) stitches using the knit-on cast-on method (see page 32). Work in stockinette stitch (knit 1 row, purl 1 row, repeat) for 2 inches. Change to the larger needles and continue in stockinette stitch until the piece measures 21 (23, 25, 26) inches. Measure with the edge curled about 2 inches—don't pull it flat to measure it. Bind off 19 (22, 24, 27) stitches at the beginning of the next 2 rows. Place the remaining stitches on a holder.

picking up
dropped stitches

Sometimes while you are knitting you will accidentally drop a stitch off 1 of your needles and it will begin to unravel downward. Instead of a stitch you will see a bar of yarn with a loose stitch (that looks like a loop) below it. If you have dropped more than 1 stitch the bars will look like a ladder. At the bottom of the ladder you will find the loose stitch.

To correct this problem on a **knit row**, knit to the point where the dropped stitch (or stitches) is located. Insert a crochet hook up into the loose stitch. Catch the bar directly above it with the hook and pull it through the opening in the loose stitch. Repeat if there is more than 1 dropped stitch. Transfer the stitch on the crochet hook to the knitting needle.

To correct this problem on a **purl row**, turn the work around so that the knit side is facing you, following the directions for correcting a dropped stitch on a knit row, then turn the work around again so the purl side is facing you.

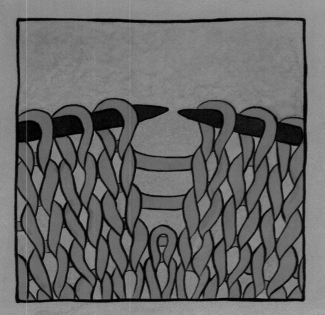
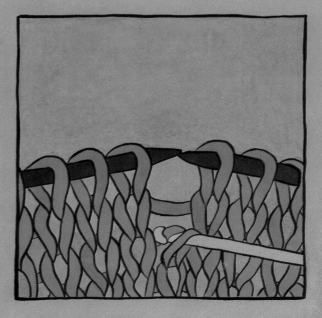

new technique for decreasing

You may have noticed that when you decrease by knitting 2 stitches together (as for the shaping of the left neck edge of the Curly-Edge Pullover) the decrease slants to the right. When you want a decrease to slant to the left (as for the right neck edge), you need to use a different method of decreasing. In the Curly-Edge Pullover pattern it is written as "knit 1, slip 1, knit 1, pass the slipped stitch over." In knitting shorthand, it might also be written as "k1, sl1, k1, psso." Here is a breakdown of what this means:

Knit 1 (k1): Knit this stitch as usual.

Slip 1 (sl1): Without changing the position of your working yarn (it should be in back), insert your right needle up into the center of the next stitch on your left needle as if you are going to knit it, but instead of knitting it, simply transfer it to your right needle.

Knit 1 (k1): Knit this stitch as usual.

Pass the Slipped Stitch Over (psso): Gently holding the top knit stitch on your right needle in place with your right forefinger, insert your left needle down into the center of the slipped stitch on the right needle and lift the slipped stitch over the knit stitch so that it comes off the right needle. This is the same action you use when you bind off.

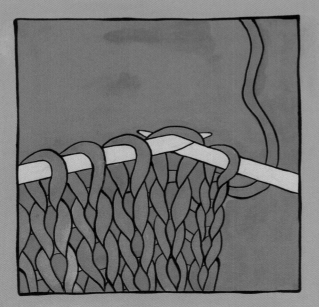
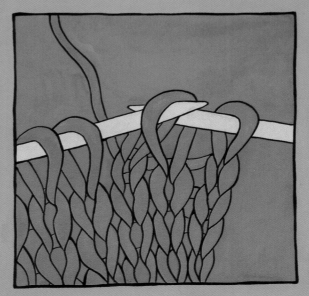

to make the front

Work as for the back until the piece measures 18½ (20½, 22½, 23½) inches, ending after you have completed a wrong-side (purl) row. Measure with the edge curled as for the back of the sweater. In the next row, knit 25 (28, 30, 33) stitches, place the remaining stitches on a holder, and purl back on the stitches that are not on the holder.

Shape the left neck edge as follows:
Row 1 (right side): Knit until 3 stitches remain; decrease 1 by knitting 2 together, then knit 1.
Row 2 (wrong side): Purl all stitches.
Repeat rows 1 and 2 until 19 (22, 24, 27) stitches remain. Work back and forth on these stitches until the front is the same as the back in length. Bind off all stitches on the right side. Place the center 15 stitches on a holder. Place the remaining 25 (28, 30, 33) stitches onto the needle. Join yarn and knit 1 row on the right side, turn, and purl back.

Shape the right neck edge as follows:
Row 1 (right side): Knit 1, slip 1, knit 1, pass the slipped stitch over. See page 118 for an explanation of this new technique for decreasing. Knit to the end of the row.
Row 2 (wrong side): Purl all stitches. Repeat rows 1 and 2 until 19 (22, 24, 27) stitches remain. Work back and forth on these stitches until the front is the same as the back in length. Bind off all stitches on the right (knit) side.

Blocking

For best results, the individual pieces of the Curly-Edge Pullover (or any handknit sweater) should be blocked before they are sewn together. That means that each piece should be dampened and pinned out to dry in the desired shape and size. The process of blocking will smooth out the stitches and help to give the sweater a professional, finished look. There are a few different ways to block a sweater. The method below is 1 of the simplest.

Lay a large bath towel on a flat surface. Place the front, back, and sleeves of the Curly-Edge Pullover on the towel, right (knit) side down. Smooth out the pieces and pin them to the towel so that the measurements match the finished measurements listed for your size at the beginning of the pattern. Do not pin the bottoms of the Curly-Edge Pullover pieces where they are meant to curl (about 2 inches of knitting should be left to curl). Cover the pinned areas of each piece with damp dish towels and let them sit overnight, or until the dish towels and the sweater pieces are completely dry.

Picking Up Stitches

To make the neckline on the Curly-Edge Pullover, you have to pick up stitches along the entire neck opening as follows: Pick up 11 stitches along the left front neck edge by inserting your knitting needle under 2 out of every 3 stitches (pick up 2, skip 1), as shown in the illustration. Next, slip the 15 stitches from the holder at the center front onto the needle. Now pick up 11 stitches along the right front neck edge as you did for the left front neck edge. Finally, slip the 27 stitches from the holder at the center back onto the needle. You now have a total of 64 stitches on your needle and are ready to start knitting the collar in the round.

to make the sleeves

With the smaller needles, cast on 24 (28, 31, 35) stitches. Work in stockinette stitch (knit 1 row, purl 1 row, repeat) for 2 inches. Change to the larger needles and continue in stockinette stitch, increasing 1 stitch 2 stitches in from the edge on each side on the 1st and every following 4th (4th, 6th, 6th) row until you have 52 (56, 59, 63) stitches. Continue until the sleeve measures 14 (15, 16, 17) inches or the length you want it to be. Be sure to measure with the edge curled about an inch. Bind off all stitches. Make a second sleeve to match the first one.

finishing

Following the instructions on page 119, block the pieces, then sew together the shoulder seams using the overcast stitch. Measure down 7½ (8, 8½, 9) inches from the shoulder seam on the front and back and run an approximately 6-inch piece of yarn through the edge of the knitted fabric at that point. This yarn will act as a marker and should be removed once you have sewn the sleeves to the body. Sew the sleeves to the body between the markers using the overcast stitch, matching the center of the sleeve to the shoulder seam. Sew the side and sleeve seams using the mattress stitch.

to make the collar

With the circular needle, pick up 11 stitches along the left front (see illustration at left); slip the 15 stitches from the holder at the center front onto the needle; pick up 11 stitches from right front; then slip the 27 stitches from the back neck holder onto the needle. You should have a total of 64 stitches on your needle. Working in the round, knit until the collar measures 3 inches or the desired length. Bind off loosely. Allow the collar to roll. Weave in any ends.

reading a knitting pattern

The knitting patterns in this book are written for beginners. The detailed style used here is different from the style used for standard knitting patterns, which are full of special abbreviations that can make them look as though they were written in a secret code. Sometimes people don't even try to knit because all the abbreviations make the instructions look scary. That's too bad. Here's a list of some of the most common abbreviations. If you are ever following knitting instructions and you come across an abbreviation that is not included here and you cannot figure it out, find an experienced knitter to ask. Don't stop knitting!

common abbreviations

approx	approximately	**meas**	measures	**St st**	stockinette stitch
alt	alternate	**m**	meter(s)	**tbl**	through back loop(s)
beg	beginning	**MC**	main color	**tog**	together
BO	bind off	**oz**	ounce(s)	**WS**	wrong side(s)
CC	contrasting color	**p**	purl	**wyib**	with yarn in back
cn	cable needle	**patt(s)**	pattern(s)	**wyif**	with yarn in front
CO	cast on	**psso**	pass slip stitch(es) over	**yds**	yards
cont	continue/continuing	**rem**	remains/remaining	**yo**	yarn over needle
dec	decrease/decreasing	**rep**	repeat	**"**	inches
dpn	double-pointed needle(s)	**RH**	right-hand	*****	repeat directions following*
foll	follow(s)/following	**RS**	right side(s)		(or between *'s) as many
g	gram(s)	**rnd(s)**	rounds		times as indicated
inc	increase/increasing	**sl**	slip	**[ ]**	repeat directions inside
k	knit	**sl st**	slip stitch		brackets as many times
LH	left-hand	**ssk**	slip, slip, knit		as indicated
lp(s)	loop(s)	**st(s)**	stitch(es)		

Now see if you can understand the following sample instructions:

With size 10½ needles and 1 (4-oz) skein (approx 125 yds) bulky yarn, CO 72 stitches. Work in St st until your work measures 8". Dec as foll: Row 1: K2 tog; rep all the way across (36 sts rem). Row 2: Purl. Rows 3 and 4: Rep rows 1 and 2 (18 sts rem). Row 5: Rep row 1 (9 sts rem). Cut yarn and thread end through rem 9 sts, pull to tighten. Sew seam.

If you follow these instructions, you will end up with a Curly-Edge Cap to go with your Curly-Edge Pullover. It will look like Sasha's red cap on page 114.

shopping for yarn

All the different colors and kinds of yarn sold in stores represent the choices you have as a knitter. This makes shopping for yarn exciting—but sometimes confusing. Remember that some yarns are best suited to specific purposes. For example, a fine cotton yarn will work well if you are knitting a lace tablecloth, but it is not the best choice for a winter sweater. Most patterns will suggest a specific type of yarn, and the salespeople at yarn shops are also available to answer your questions. The next few pages tell you where to find the yarns used in this book and how to wash and store your finished creations.

list of yarns

Here is a list of the exact yarns used for the projects in this book.

All Bean Bags
(pages 34, 71, and 106)
Classic Elite Artisan bulky yarn
(90% wool and 10% alpaca)
1 (3½-ounce) skein measures
approximately 127 yards and makes
approximately 4 bean bags
Shown in assorted colors

Pocket Scarf & Hat Set
(pages 38 and 43)
Tahki Cottage bulky wool yarn
1 (1¾-ounce) ball measures about
68 yards
5-color version: 4 balls Gold (#573),
1 ball Purple (#571), 1 ball Pink (#579),
1 ball Green (#574), and 1 ball
Teal (#572)
2-color version: 5 balls Blue (#580) and
2 balls Red (#576)

Patchwork Afghan
(pages 44 and 47)
Classic Elite Artisan bulky yarn
(90% wool and 10% alpaca)
Full-size afghan shown in Crocheter's
Ocean Blue (#2357), Painter's Pink
(#2371), Gardener's Geranium (#2358),
Herbalist Moss (#2381), and
Beekeeper's Gold (#2309)
Doll-size afghan shown in Stonemason
Slate (#2349) and Arborist's Green
(#2372)
1 (3½-ounce) skein measures
approximately 127 yards and will make
approximately 1½ 12-inch squares or
3 6-inch squares

Garter Stitch Dolls
(pages 52 and 58)
Schoolhouse Press Highland Wool
bulky yarn
1 (4-ounce) skein measures approximately
175 yards and will make 1 doll or 2 vests
Dolls shown in Honey Beige, Acorn
(dark brown), and Sorrel (light brown);
vest shown in Burnt Orange

Owl & Pussycat Bath Puppets
(page 60)
Classic Elite Sand Cotton bulky yarn
1 (3½-ounce) skein measures about
154 yards and will make approximately
2½ puppets
Shown in Spring Green (#6435),
Ultramarine/dark blue (#6493),
Tuscan Olive (#6474), Weeping
Wisteria/light blue (#6414), Portuguese
Turquoise (#6404), and Rouge
Vif D'Etames/bright orange (#6498)

Crazy Caterpillar (pages 66 and 72)
Classic Elite Artisan bulky yarn (90% wool
and 10% alpaca)
1 (3½-ounce) skein measures
approximately 127 yards; approximately
¼ skein of each color needed to make a
14-inch caterpillar
Shown in Illustrator's Ink (#2313), Herbalist's Moss (#2381), Crocheter's Ocean
Blue (#2357), and Painter's Pink (#2371)

Wraparound Ribbed Scarf (page 76)
3-Strand Morehouse Merino
1 (2-ounce) skein measures
approximately 145 yards
2 or 3 skeins needed to make 1 scarf
Shown in Silver

Backpack & More (pages 84 and 89)
Rowan Recycled Chunky (blue backpack)
and Rowan Chunky Tweed (brown backpack) bulky wool yarn
1 (3½-ounce) skein measures approximately 110 yards; 2 skeins of main color
and 1 skein of contrasting color needed
to make backpack and accessories
Shown in Recycled Chunky in Steel (#898)
and Rags (#897) and Chunky Tweed in
Marmalade (#883) and Weasel (#894)

Wizard's Cap (pages 90, 92, and 111)
Classic Elite Tapestry worsted-weight
wool yarn
1 (1¾-ounce) skein measures
approximately 95 yards; 2 skeins needed
to make child- or adult-sized cap
Shown in assorted colors

Magic Spiral Tube Socks
(pages 78, 94, and 96)
Classic Elite Tapestry worsted-weight
wool yarn
1 (1¾-ounce) skein measures
approximately 95 yards; 3 skeins
needed to make 1 pair of child- or
adult-sized socks
Shown in assorted colors

Swatch Scarf
(pages 102 and 104)
Classic Elite Montera bulky yarn
(50% wool and 50% alpaca)
1 3½-ounce skein measures
approximately 127 yards
Shown in Laguna del Luna Blue (#3857),
Lake Titicaca Turquoise (#3831),
Rainforest Green (#3874), Tropical
Forest Green (#3802), and Bolivian
Wildflower (#3888)

Curly-Edge Pullover
(pages 112 and 114)
Brown Sheep Company Lamb's Pride
Bulky wool yarn (to make all pullovers
except for the white one) or Morehouse
Farm Wind Dancer Merino bulky wool yarn
(to make the white pullover)
1 (4-ounce skein) Lambs Pride Bulky
measures 125 yards; 7 (8, 9, 10) skeins
(depending on size) needed to make 1
pullover (buy 1 extra skein if making
sweater with stripes in 3 or more colors)
Solid color pullover made with Blue Blood
Red (M80)
3-color striped pullover made with Aztec
Turquoise (M78), Winter Blue (M51), and
Seafoam (M16)
5-color striped pullover made with Sun-
burst Gold (M14), Rust (M97), Blue
Heirloom (M75), Raspberry (M83), and
Old Sage (M69)
1 (3½-ounce) skein Morehouse Farm
Wind Dancer Merino measures 190 yards;
5 (6, 7, 8) skeins needed to make 1
pullover (depending on size)

finding the yarn and tools featured in this book

Here are the names and addresses of the companies that sell the yarn and tools featured in this book, plus 2 mail-order companies that sell all sorts of knitting and related merchandise. Write or call for the names of stores in your area and for mail-order catalogs.

Brown Sheep Yarn Company
100662 County Road 16
Mitchell, NE 69357
800-826-9136

Classic Elite Yarns
300A Jackson Street
Lowell, MA 01852
800-343-0308

Morehouse Farm Sheep's Clothing
2 Rock City Road
Milan, NY 12571
845-758-6493

One World Button Supply Company
41 Union Square West, Room 311
New York, NY 10003
212-691-1331

Patternworks (mail-order catalog)
P.O. Box 1618
Center Harbor, NH 03226
800-438-5464
*for yarn, tools, and unspun wool

Rowan Yarns
Westminster Fibers
4 Townsend West/Unit 8
Nashua, NH 03063
800-445-9276

Schoolhouse Press
6899 Cary Bluff
Pittsville, WI 54466
800-968-5648

Tahki Stacy Charles Yarns
8000 Cooper Avenue
Building 1
Glendale, NY 11385
718-326-4433

**The Wool Connection
(mail-order catalog)**
34 East Main Street
Old Avon Village North
Avon, CT 06001
800-933-9665
*for yarn, tools, and unspun wool

sample letter

Your Name
Street Address
City, State, Zip Code
Phone Number

Company Name
Street Address
City, State, Zip Code

Dear Company Name,

I am _____ years old. I read about your company in *Kids Knitting* by Melanie Falick and I am interested in buying some of your yarn, but I do not know where I can buy it locally. I would appreciate it very much if you would send me the names and addresses of stores in my area where your yarn is sold. I would also like to know about any mail-order sources.

Thank you very much.

Yours sincerely,

Sign Your Name
Print Your Name

caring for your handknits

washing

Most synthetic fibers, such as acrylic, can be washed in a machine. Natural fibers, such as wool, usually need to be washed by hand. Care information is usually printed on the yarn label. If you are unsure, always handwash to avoid mistakes. Wool does not absorb stains or odors easily: A drop of food can often be removed from a wool garment by wiping it gently with a wet cloth and many odors will fade away if a wool garment is allowed to hang overnight on the back of a chair in a room with good circulation. When washing a wool garment, buy a cleaning product designed for this purpose and follow the instructions on the label or those below.

1. Fill a bathtub or basin with lukewarm (not cold or hot) water. Add the amount of soap specified by the manufacturer or enough to create a small amount of suds. Place your garment in the water and gently squeeze and move it around. Do not rub or twist the fabric because these rough actions will cause the fibers to felt. Let the garment soak in the tub or basin for about 10 minutes.

2. Very gently squeeze the garment to remove the sudsy water, then lift the garment from the tub or basin and refill it with fresh, lukewarm rinse water. Immerse the garment in the water, then gently squeeze again. Continue this process until no suds remain, always using water that is the same temperature. (Changing the temperature of the water will "shock" the fibers and also cause felting.)

3. Lay a thick, dry towel on the floor and place the garment flat on top of it. Roll up the towel with the garment in it and gently press on it. The towel will absorb water from the garment.

4. If you have a washing machine (and an adult's assistance or permission to run it by yourself), remove more of the water by using the spin cycle: Place the garment in a pillowcase, secure it shut with a tight knot or a strip of scrap fabric, and place it in the washing machine by itself. Set the machine on the spin cycle and run it for a few minutes. (It is important that the pillowcase does not open during this process.)

5. To finish drying the garment, lay it flat on a dry towel placed on a flat, water-resistant surface away from direct sunlight, indoor heat sources (such as a radiator), and pets. Arrange the garment into its normal shape and let it sit until dry.

storing

Clean handknits should be folded and stored on a shelf in a closet, in a dresser drawer, or in a sweater chest. Do not place handknits on hangers because they will stretch out of shape. To protect handknits made with natural fibers from moths, store them with a sachet filled with dried, strong-smelling herbs (such as lavender and rosemary) or cedar chips. Most important, make sure when you put sweaters away for the season that they are clean. Moths definitely prefer dirty handknits to clean ones.

index

acknowledgments

Lots of people worked very hard to put *Kids Knitting* together. Kristin Nicholas not only painted all of the illustrations in this book (a gigantic job), she also designed the Patchwork Afghan and Owl and Pussycat Bath Puppets. The other designers were Barbara Albright (Polka-Dot Knitting Needles, Bean Bags, Crazy Caterpillar, and Swatch Scarf); Pam Allen (Wizard's Cap, Magic Spiral Tube Socks); Sue Flanders (Garter Stitch Dolls); and Julie Hoff (Pocket Hat and Scarf, Backpack & More, and Curly-Edge Pullover). Knitters Mary K. Cox, Anne Hanson, Diana Waill (my mom), and Katie Gunter knit extra samples for photography. Margrit Lohrer and Albrecht Pichler welcomed us at Morehouse Farm, where Chris Hartlove took all of the photographs; Hamish Wallace was a big help to Chris during the photo shoot. The models were Sasha Erber-Pearl, Manon Hutton-DeWys, Stanley Grayson, Emily Katz, Molly Lundquist-Baz, Nick Stoker, and Abigail Wallace. Ann Alexander and Mary Stowe organized special kids' knitting classes for me to teach at Yarns, etc., and Fiber Space in North Carolina. Stephanie Gray, Courtney Bulla, Nikki Mills, Andrew Gamble, Sierra Dickey, Emma Schall, Betina Van Denend, Mattie Whitmore, and Hannah Gordon were my students there. Mary Jane Mucklestone, the knitting teacher at the Waldorf School in Rockland, Maine, gave me the idea for the Acorn Knitting Needles, and she and her students welcomed me at their school. Dee Neer checked all of the technical illustrations and instructions. Barbara Clark copyedited the manuscript. Susi Oberhelman designed the book. Agent Sallie Gouverneur and my editors, Leslie Stoker and Siobhán McGowan, guided me wisely. Thank you everyone.